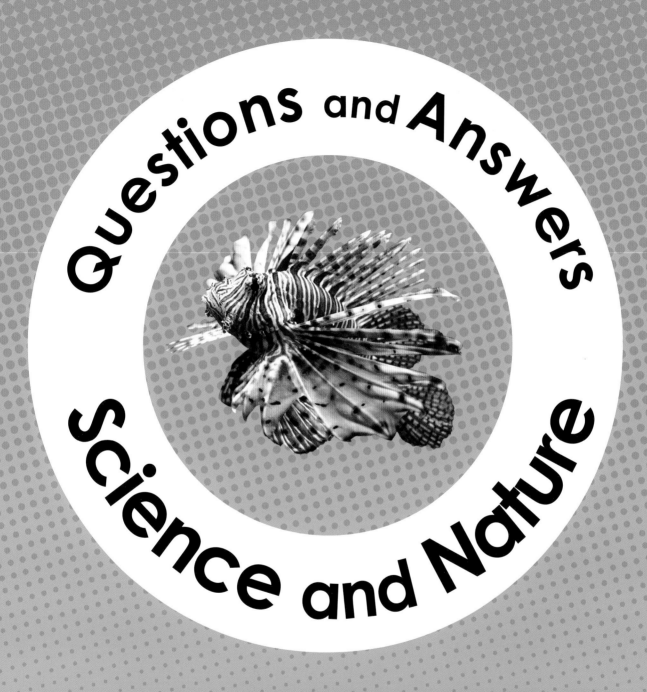

Questions and Answers

Science and Nature

An Imprint of Sterling Publishing
387 Park Avenue South
New York, NY 10016

Writter by: John Farndon, Anita Ganeri, Jen Green, Lucinda Hawksley, Ian Janes, Jinny Johnson, Claudia Martin, Malcolm Penny, Joyce Pope, Angela Royston, Philip Steele, John Stidworthy, and Martin Walters

Consultants: Sarah Durant, Benjamin Robinson, Ade Scott Colson, Tony Sizer, and Astrid Wingler

Americanizer: Michael Jones
Proofreader: Joanne Brooks

ISBN 978-1-4351-4352-4

Manufactured 05/12
Lot #10 9 8 7 6 5 4 3 2 1

Cover images: front t iStockphoto.com

Questions and Answers
Science and Nature

Sandy Creek
NEW YORK

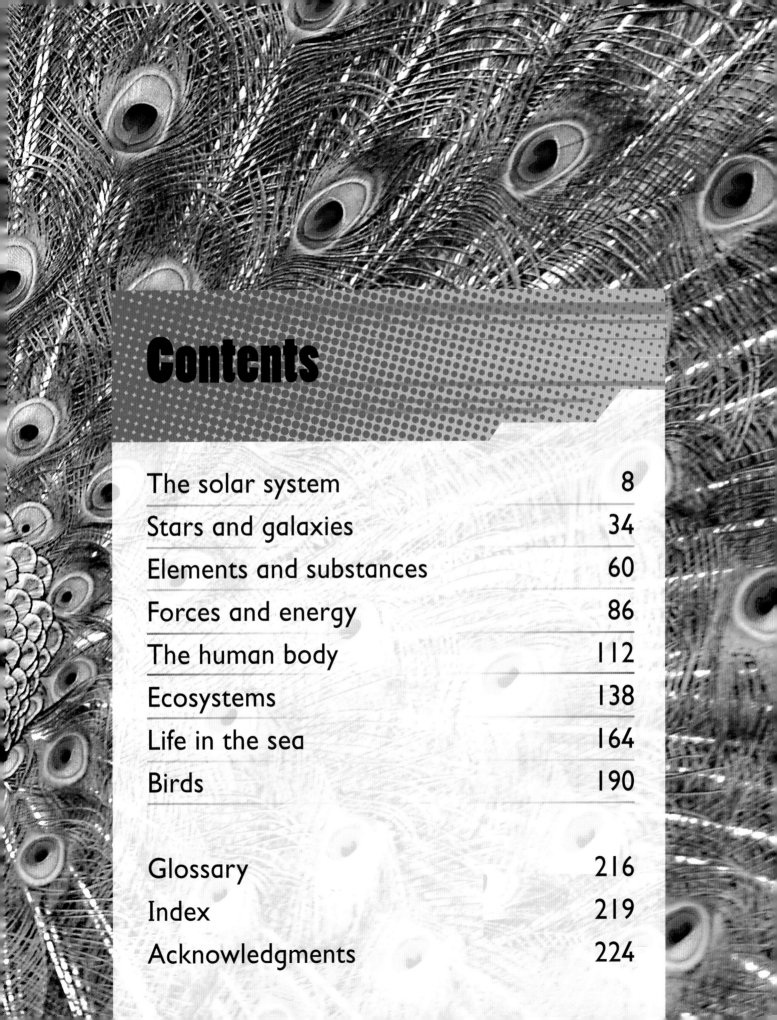

Contents

WHY DO CRABS WALK SIDEWAYS?

WHY DO BIRDS SING?

WHERE ARE STARS

HOW BIG ARE ATOMS?

HOW DOES GRAVITY HOL

HOW DOES BREAD RISE?

WHAT

HOW LONG CAN YOU HOLD

WHY DO YOUR EARS POP?

WHICH FISH CAN

HOW OLD IS THE SUN?

WHY IS NEPTUNE GREEN?

WHAT WAS THE BIG BANG?

BORN?

D YOU DOWN?

WHAT IS AN OASIS?

DO WE GET FROM RAIN FORESTS?

YOUR BREATH?

WHAT ARE GENES

WALK ON LAND?

Introduction

Did you ever wonder if there is life on other planets? Or how black holes are formed? Do you know why the sky is blue? Or what makes your blood red? Have you ever wanted to know which is the hottest, driest desert? Or which shark is the most deadly killing machine? In this book, you will find out the answers to 555 amazing questions you've always wanted to ask—covering everything from atoms to X-rays, from flying fish to flightless birds, from strangler figs to living stones, from tongues to intestines.

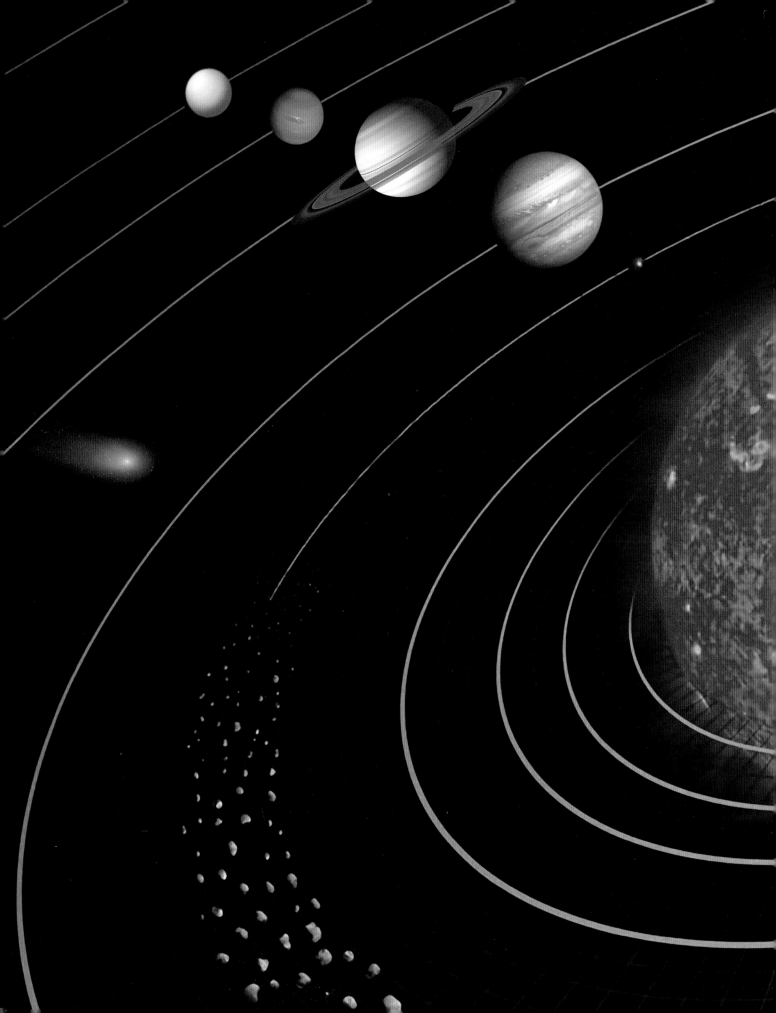

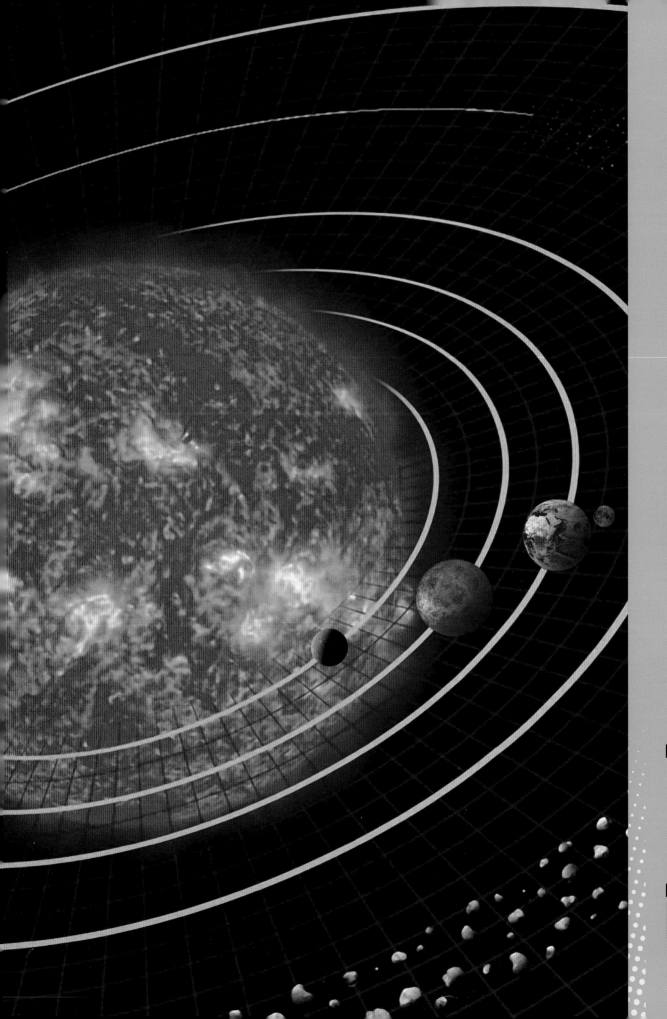

The solar system

Formation of Earth >

Our planet has not always existed. In fact, Earth is a relatively young planet. Scientists believe that the universe may be 13.7 billion years old. But Earth—along with the rest of our solar system—was born only about 4.6 billion years ago.

PLANET BIRTH

Our solar system formed from a gas and dust cloud.

TOP QUESTION ?

HOW DID EARTH BEGIN?

Around 4.6 billion years ago, a cloud of gas and dust swirled around our newly formed Sun. Gradually, the grains of dust and gas were pulled together into clumps by their own gravity. These clumps became the Earth and the other planets in our solar system.

SOLAR SYSTEM

Scientists have built up a picture of our solar system's birth, as the planets were slowly formed around the Sun.

> HOW BIG IS THE EARTH?

Satellite measurements show it is 24,901 miles around the equator and 7,926 miles across. The diameter between the poles is slightly less, by 27 miles.

> WHAT WAS EARLY EARTH LIKE?

Early Earth was a fiery ball. It took half a billion years for its surface to cool and form a hard crust. As it cooled, Earth gave off gases and water vapor, which formed the atmosphere.

WHAT IS EARTH MADE OF?

Earth has a core consisting mostly of iron and a rocky crust made mostly of oxygen and silicon. In between is the soft, hot mantle of metal silicates, sulfides, and oxides.

Crust

Core

Mantle

WHAT SHAPE IS EARTH?

Earth is not quite a perfect sphere. The spinning of the planet causes it to bulge at the equator. Scientists describe Earth's shape as "geoid," which simply means Earth-shaped! The poles, Earth's most northerly and southerly spots, are the points Earth spins around.

HOW OLD ARE OCEANS?

The oceans were formed between 4.2 and 3.8 billion years ago. As the earth cooled, clouds of steam became water, creating vast oceans.

OLD ROCK

Earth's oldest rock is about 3.8 billion years old.

Our special planet >

Earth is the largest of the four inner planets, which lie closest to the Sun and are mostly made of rock. These four planets are Mercury, Venus, Earth, and Mars, with our planet being third from the Sun. Earth is the only planet in the universe on which life is known to exist.

> HOW LONG IS A DAY?

A day is the time Earth takes to turn once. The stars move to the same place in the sky every 23 hours, 56 minutes, and 4.09 seconds (the sidereal day). Our day (the solar day) is 24 hours, because Earth is moving around the Sun, and must turn an extra 1 degree for the Sun to be in the same place in the sky.

> DOES EARTH SPIN?

Earth spins on its axis once a day, while also orbiting, or traveling around, the Sun.

SUMMER AND WINTER

As Earth orbits the Sun, the hemisphere of the planet tilted toward the Sun has its summer.

❯ HOW LONG IS A YEAR?

Earth travels around the Sun every 365.24 days, which gives us our calendar year of 365 days. To make up the extra 0.24 days, we add an extra day to our calendar at the end of February in every fourth year, which is called the leap year—and then we have to get rid of a leap year every four centuries.

❯ WHAT'S SPECIAL ABOUT EARTH?

Earth is the only planet where temperatures are right for liquid water to exist on the surface. It is also the only planet with oxygen in its atmosphere. Both water and oxygen are needed for life to exist.

❯ WHAT IS THE ATMOSPHERE?

Earth's atmosphere, or "air," is a layer of gases—including nitrogen, oxygen, argon, and carbon dioxide—that surrounds the planet.

WHO WAS COPERNICUS?

In the 1500s, most people thought Earth was fixed in the center of the universe, with the Sun and the stars revolving around it. Nicolaus Copernicus (1473–1543) was the Polish astronomer who first suggested Earth was moving around the Sun.

SUNSET

Earth turns on its axis once every 24 hours, so the Sun appears to rise in the east and move across the sky to set in the west.

The Moon

The Moon is Earth's natural satellite. Natural satellites, or moons, are objects that orbit a planet or other body in space. Our Moon is a rocky ball about a quarter of Earth's diameter. It is held in its orbit around Earth by gravity.

> WHAT IS THE MOON?

The Moon has circled Earth for at least 4 billion years. Most scientists believe that the Moon formed when, early in Earth's history, a planet smashed into it. The impact was so great that nothing was left of the planet but a few splashes thrown back up into space. These splashes and material from the battered Earth were drawn together by gravity to form the Moon.

MOON DUST

The Moon's surface is covered with a fine layer of dust. Beneath lies a crust of rock.

ARE THERE OTHER MOONS?

As many as 240 bodies, all in our solar system, are classified as moons. Other stars and their planets are likely to have moons, but none has yet been observed.

WHAT IS MOONLIGHT?

The Moon is by far the brightest thing in the night sky. But it has no light of its own. Moonlight is simply the Sun's light reflected off the dust on the Moon's surface.

TOP ? QUESTION

WHAT ARE TIDES?

Tides are caused by the oceans on the side of Earth facing the Moon being pulled by the Moon's gravity more than the solid Earth itself. On the opposite side of Earth, the water is actually pulled less than Earth. This creates a bulge of water on each side of the world. This bulge stays under the Moon as Earth turns.

TIDES

As Earth spins, the Moon's gravity makes the oceans rise.

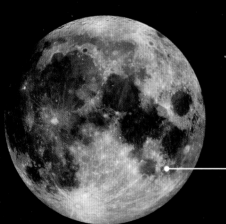

LUNAR SEAS

People once thought these dark patches were filled with water. In fact, they are formed from lava.

WHY DOES THE MOON HAVE CRATERS?

The Moon's surface is covered with impact craters. These form when asteroids and comets crash into the Moon. Most of the craters were made about 3–4 billion years ago.

WHAT ARE THE MOON'S SEAS?

The dark patches on the Moon's surface are called seas, but in fact they are not seas at all. They were formed about 3 billion years ago when lava from inside the Moon flowed into huge craters and then solidified.

Our nearest neighbor ➤

HUMAN VISITORS

This footprint was made on the Moon's surface during the Apollo 11 mission.

As the brightest object in the night sky, the Moon has always fascinated humankind. We have made up stories to explain it and built telescopes to observe it. The Moon is the only celestial body—or object in space—upon which humans have landed.

➤ WHO WERE THE FIRST PEOPLE ON THE MOON?

The first men on the Moon were Neil Armstrong and Buzz Aldrin of the U.S. Apollo 11 mission. They landed on the Moon on 20 July, 1969. As Armstrong set foot on the Moon, he said, "That's one small step for (a) man, one giant leap for mankind."

LUNAR ECLIPSE

As the Moon passes through Earth's shadow, the Sun's blue light is scattered by Earth's atmosphere. The remaining red light is refracted, or bent, into Earth's shadow. This makes the Moon appear red.

PHASES OF THE MOON

The Moon appears to wax (grow) and shrink (wane) every 29.53 days, as we see its sunny side from different angles.

❯ WHAT IS WAXING?

Over the first two weeks of each month, we see more and more of the Moon's bright side until it is a full moon. As the Moon appears to grow, we say that it is waxing.

TOP QUESTION

WHAT IS A NEW MOON?

The Moon appears to change shape during the month because, as it circles Earth, we see its bright, sunny side from a different angle. At the new moon, the Moon lies between Earth and the Sun, and we catch only a crescent-shape glimpse of its bright side.

❯ HOW LONG IS A MONTH?

It takes the Moon 27.3 days to circle Earth, but 29.53 days from one full moon to the next, because Earth is moving as well. A lunar month is the 29.53 days cycle. Our calendar months are entirely artificial.

❯ WHAT IS A LUNAR ECLIPSE?

As the Moon goes around Earth, sometimes it passes right into Earth's shadow, where sunlight is blocked off. This is a lunar eclipse. If you look at the Moon during this time, you can see the dark disk of Earth's shadow creeping across the Moon.

❯ WHAT IS A HARVEST MOON?

The harvest moon is the full moon nearest to the September equinox (when night and day are of equal length). This moon hangs bright above the eastern horizon for several evenings, providing a good light for farmers harvesting their crops.

The Sun >

The Sun is the star at the center of our solar system. Earth and the other planets orbit the Sun, which makes up 99 percent of the solar system's mass. Sunlight and heat from the Sun support all life on Earth. Without the Sun, there would be no life at all.

> WHAT IS THE SUN?

The Sun is an average star, just like countless others in the universe. It was formed from a cloud of gas and dust, plus material thrown out by one or more exploding stars. Now, in middle age, the Sun burns yellow and quite steadily—giving Earth daylight and fairly constant temperatures. Besides heat and light, the Sun sends out deadly gamma rays, X-rays, and ultraviolet, as well as infrared and radio waves.

THE BOILING SURFACE

The Sun's visible surface is called the photosphere. It is a sea of boiling gas that gives the heat and light we experience on Earth.

> WHAT MAKES THE SUN BURN?

The Sun gets its heat from nuclear fusion. Huge pressures deep inside the Sun force the nuclei (cores) of hydrogen atoms to fuse together to make helium atoms, releasing vast amounts of nuclear energy.

WHAT IS A SOLAR ECLIPSE?

A solar eclipse is when the Moon moves in between the Sun and Earth (shown on the left), creating a shadow a few hundred miles wide on Earth.

HOW BIG IS THE SUN?

The Sun is a small- to medium-size star 865,000 miles in diameter. It weighs just under 2,200 trillion trillion tons.

MERCURY IN TRANSIT

The last transit of Mercury took place on 8 November, 2006.

WHAT IS A TRANSIT?

Mercury and Venus are the two planets closer to the Sun than Earth. Occasionally, they can be seen crossing, or in transit over, the face of the Sun. Mercury crosses 13 or 14 times a century; Venus crosses twice every 120 years.

WHAT IS THE SUN'S CROWN?

The Sun's crown is its corona, its glowing white hot atmosphere. It is seen only as a halo when the rest of the Sun's disk is blotted out by the moon in a solar eclipse.

ECLIPSE

During an eclipse, the Moon's shadow can be seen on Earth. Up to five eclipses occur each year.

Ball of fire >

While the solar system orbits the Sun, the Sun itself is orbiting the center of our Galaxy, the Milky Way. The Sun is moving at an orbital speed of 156 miles every second. It takes the solar system about 225 to 250 million years to complete one orbit of the Galaxy.

LIGHT DISPLAY

The northern lights often appear as a greenish glow or a faint red. They can occur as arcs or bands.

> WHAT IS THE SOLAR WIND?

The solar wind is the stream of particles constantly blowing out from the Sun at hundreds of miles per second. Earth is protected from the solar wind by its magnetic field, but at the poles the solar wind interacts with Earth's atmosphere to create the *aurora borealis,* or Northern Lights, and the *aurora australis,* or Southern Lights.

> HOW HOT IS THE SUN?

The surface of the Sun is a phenomenal 9,900°F, and would melt absolutely anything. But its core is thousands of times hotter at over 27 million°F!

> HOW OLD IS THE SUN?

The Sun is a middle-age star. It probably formed about 4.6 billion years ago. It will probably burn for another 5 billion years and then die in a blaze so bright that Earth will be scorched right out of existence.

➤ WHAT ARE SUNSPOTS?

Sunspots are dark blotches seen on the Sun's surface (right). They are thousands of miles across, and usually occur in pairs. They are dark because they are slightly less hot than the rest of the surface. As the Sun rotates, they slowly cross its face—in about 31 days at the equator and 27 days at the poles.

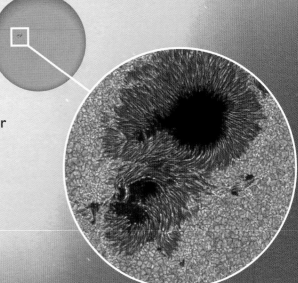

➤ WHAT IS THE SOLAR CYCLE?

The average number of sunspots and flares seems to reach a maximum every 11 years. Some scientists think that these peaks in the Sun's cycle are linked to stormier weather on Earth.

TOP QUESTION

WHAT ARE SOLAR FLARES?

Flares are eruptions on the Sun's surface that release energy into space with the power of one million atom bombs for about five minutes. Solar prominences are giant flamelike tongues of hot hydrogen that loop up to 20,000 miles into space.

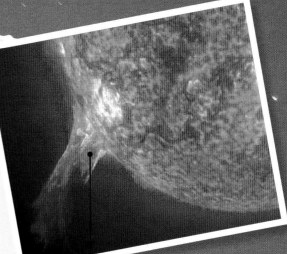

SOLAR PROMINENCE

Prominences form in about a day and may last as long as several months.

Venus and Mercury >

Along with Earth and Mars, Venus and Mercury make up the inner planets. These planets all have an atmosphere, but each is very different. Mercury orbits the Sun at a distance of 29–43 million miles, while Venus has an average distance from the Sun of 67 million miles.

> WHAT ARE THE INNER PLANETS MADE OF?

Each of the inner planets is formed a little bit like an egg—with a hard "shell" or crust of rock, a "white" or mantle of soft, semi-molten rock, and a "yolk" or core of hot, often molten, iron and nickel.

> WHAT IS THE ATMOSPHERE LIKE ON VENUS?

Venus's atmosphere would be deadly for humans. It is very deep, so the pressure on the ground is huge. It is made mainly of poisonous carbon dioxide and is also filled with clouds of sulfuric acid.

VENUS

Venus is the second brightest object in the night sky, after the Moon.

VENUS'S SURFACE

This computer-generated image was created using data supplied by the Magellan space probe.

COULD YOU BREATHE ON MERCURY?

Not without your own oxygen supply. Mercury has almost no atmosphere—just a few wisps of sodium—because gases are burned off by the nearby Sun.

HOW HOT IS MERCURY?

Temperatures on Mercury veer from one extreme to the other because it has too thin an atmosphere to insulate it. In the day, temperatures soar to 750°F; at night they plunge to -280°F.

HAVE ANY SPACECRAFT VISITED MERCURY?

Only two unmanned spacecraft have been close to Mercury. Approaching the planet is difficult because it lies so close to the Sun.

TOP QUESTION

WHY IS VENUS CALLED THE EVENING STAR?

Venus reflects sunlight so well that it shines like a star. Because it is close to the Sun, we can see it in the evening, just after the Sun sets. We can also see it just before sunrise.

MERCURY

Mercury's surface is pitted with craters like the Moon. It also has mountains and valleys.

Mars >

The fourth of the inner planets is Mars, which orbits the Sun every 687 days. It is often called the "Red Planet" because of its reddish appearance. Martian temperatures range from -220°F during winter at its poles to up to 68°F during its summers.

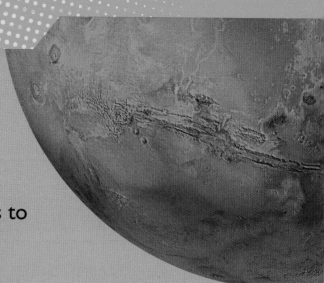

> WHY IS MARS RED?

Mars is red because it is rusty. The surface contains a high proportion of iron dust, and this has been oxidized by small amounts of oxygen in the atmosphere.

> IS THERE LIFE ON MARS?

In the 1970s, unmanned landers of the Viking missions found no trace of life. Then, in 1996, microscopic fossils of what might be miniviruses were found in a rock from Mars. But these turned out not to be signs of life after all.

MARTIAN SOIL

The soil on Mars is similar to Earth's. But the dust is often whipped up into huge dust storms that can cover the whole planet.

VALLES MARINERIS

As Mars cooled after its formation, this giant canyon opened up.

❯ WHO DISCOVERED MARS'S MOONS?

In 1877, American astronomer Asaph Hall decided to go to bed early. But his wife encouraged him to stay up and work—and that night he discovered Mars' two moons. He named them Phobos and Deimos, after the attendants of the Roman war god, Mars.

❯ WHICH CANYON IS BIGGER THAN THE GRAND CANYON?

A canyon on Mars! The planet has a great chasm, discovered by the Mariner 9 space probe and called the Valles Marineris. It is more than 2,500 miles long and four times as deep as the Grand Canyon. It is the largest known chasm in the solar system.

❯ WILL HUMANS EVER LAND ON MARS?

Both the United States and the European Space Agency have announced that they plan to send manned missions to Mars within the next 30 years.

WHERE IS THE BIGGEST VOLCANO?

Mars has a volcano called Olympus Mons, which is 17 miles high—three times higher than Mount Everest. It was created by lava welling up beneath Mars's surface.

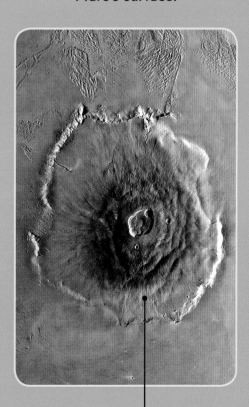

OLYMPUS MONS

This volcano is the highest mountain in the solar system and is just one of many volcanoes on the planet.

Jupiter ➤

JUPITER

High-speed winds continually whirl around Jupiter's surface, creating bands of cloud in the atmosphere.

THE MOONS

Two of Jupiter's largest moons—Io and Europa—can be seen in orbit. They are both close to the size of Earth's Moon.

The largest planet in the solar system is Jupiter, the fifth planet from the Sun. Along with Saturn, Uranus, and Neptune, Jupiter is called a gas giant. These planets do not have a solid surface because they are not made of rock or other hard materials.

➤ HOW MANY MOONS DOES JUPITER HAVE?

Jupiter has at least 63 moons. Many of them are very small— 47 are less than 6 miles in diameter. The four largest are called Io, Europa, Ganymede, and Callisto.

➤ HOW BIG IS JUPITER?

Very big. Even though Jupiter is largely gas, it weighs 320 times as much as Earth and is 88,793 miles in diameter.

WHAT IS JUPITER MADE OF?

Unlike the rocky inner planets, the gas giants are made largely of gas. Jupiter is made mostly of hydrogen and helium. Internal pressures are so great that most of the hydrogen is turned to metal.

HOW FAST DOES JUPITER SPIN?

Jupiter spins faster than any other planet. Despite its huge size, it turns around in just 9 hours 55 minutes, which means the surface is moving at 28,000 miles an hour!

COULD YOU LAND ON JUPITER?

No. Even if your spaceship could withstand the enormous pressures, there is no surface to land on—the atmosphere merges unnoticeably into deep oceans of liquid hydrogen.

IO

Io has more than 300 volcanoes, making it the most geologically active object in the solar system. Here, an eruption can be seen on its surface.

TOP ? QUESTION

WHAT IS JUPITER'S RED SPOT?

The Great Red Spot or GRS is a huge swirling storm in Jupiter's atmosphere. It is 16,000 miles across and has been going on for at least 330 years.

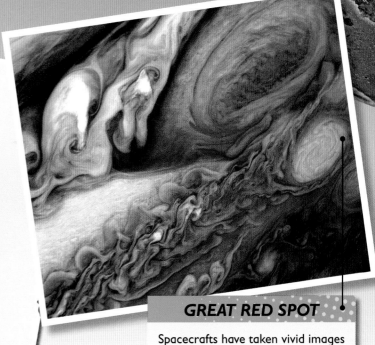

GREAT RED SPOT

Spacecrafts have taken vivid images of the storm, with its red center and wavy cloud formations.

Saturn >

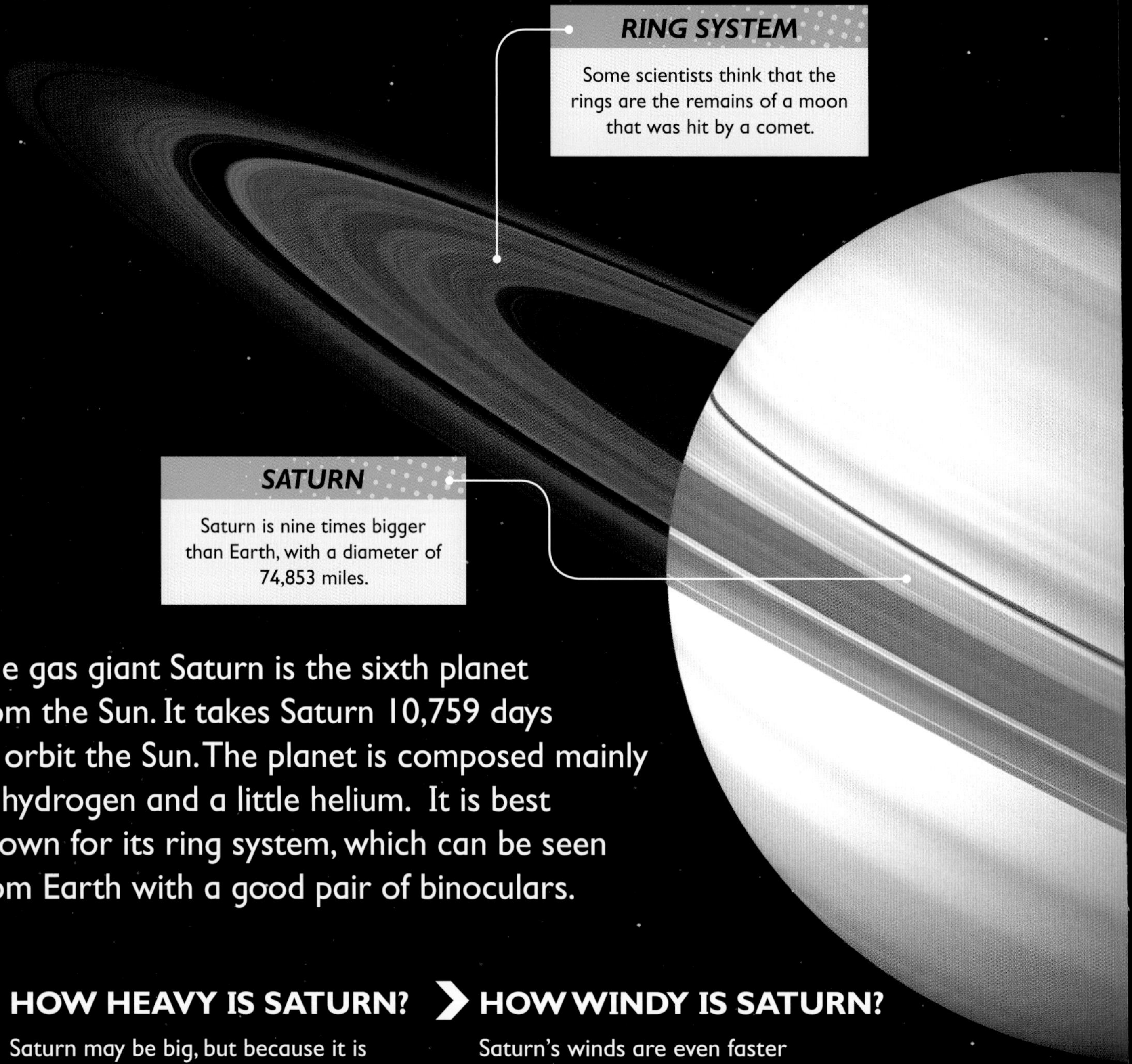

RING SYSTEM

Some scientists think that the rings are the remains of a moon that was hit by a comet.

SATURN

Saturn is nine times bigger than Earth, with a diameter of 74,853 miles.

The gas giant Saturn is the sixth planet from the Sun. It takes Saturn 10,759 days to orbit the Sun. The planet is composed mainly of hydrogen and a little helium. It is best known for its ring system, which can be seen from Earth with a good pair of binoculars.

> HOW HEAVY IS SATURN?

Saturn may be big, but because it is made largely of hydrogen, it is also remarkably light, with a mass of 660 billion trillion tons. If you could find a big enough bathtub, it would float.

> HOW WINDY IS SATURN?

Saturn's winds are even faster than Jupiter's and roar around the planet at up to 1,100 miles an hour. But Neptune's are even faster, at 1,300 miles an hour!

> ## HOW MANY MOONS DOES SATURN HAVE?

Saturn has 62 moons, including Lapetus, which is dark on one side and light on the other.

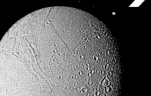

ENCELADUS

Saturn's moon Enceladus is composed of ice and rock.

> ## WHAT IS THE CASSINI DIVISION?

Saturn's rings occur in broad bands, referred to by the letters A to G. In 1675, the astronomer Cassini saw a dark gap between rings A and B. This is now called the Cassini division, after him.

> ## WHAT ARE SATURN'S RINGS?

Saturn's rings are the planet's shining halo, first seen by Galileo Galilei (1564–1642), who invented a simple telescope in 1609. The rings are incredibly thin—no more than 160 feet deep—yet they stretch 46,000 miles into space.

ICE CHIPS

The rings are made of billions of chips of ice and dust.

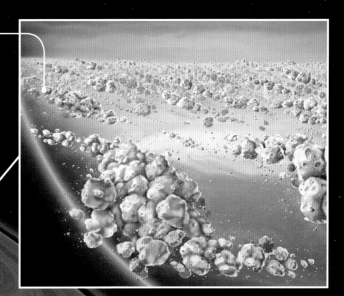

> ## WHY ARE ASTRONOMERS EXCITED ABOUT TITAN?

Saturn's moon Titan is very special because it is the only moon in the solar system with a dense atmosphere, which is vital for supporting life.

Neptune and Uranus →

Neptune and Uranus are the two planets farthest from the Sun. Like Jupiter and Saturn, they are composed mostly of gas. These two planets are sometimes known as ice giants because they contain a large amount of icy water, methane, and ammonia.

NEPTUNE

Neptune is 17 times the mass of Earth and slightly heavier than its similar sister planet, Uranus, which is only 15 times heavier.

❯ WHAT COLOR IS NEPTUNE?

Neptune appears greeny blue because of the methane gas in its atmosphere. This gas absorbs red light in the spectrum, making it seem that Neptune is a vivid, azure blue-green. The same effect can be seen with Uranus, which also has a lot of methane in its atmosphere, although that planet appears to be a much paler shade of turquoise blue.

❯ HOW LONG IS A YEAR ON NEPTUNE?

Neptune is so far from the Sun—over 2,800 million miles—that its orbit takes about 165 Earth years. So one year on Neptune lasts for 165 Earth years.

❯ WHO FOUND NEPTUNE?

Two mathematicians, John Couch Adams in England and Urbain le Verrier in France, predicted where Neptune should be from the way its gravity disturbed Uranus's orbit. Johann Galle in Berlin was the first to see it on September 23, 1846.

NEPTUNE'S WINDS

Space probes have sent back images of Neptune's high winds.

TOP QUESTION ?

▶ WHEN WAS URANUS DISCOVERED?

Uranus was first discovered in 1781 by the astronomer William Herschel. He thought at first that it was a comet, but Uranus was soon proved to be a planet.

DOES URANUS HAVE RINGS?

Like the other gas giants, Uranus has a ring system (below). Currently 13 rings have been identified.

URANUS

Uranus is the seventh planet from the Sun and is named after the Greek god of the sky.

▶ WHAT'S STRANGE ABOUT URANUS?

Unlike any of the other planets, Uranus does not spin on a slight tilt. Instead, it is tilted right over and rolls around the Sun on its side, like a giant bowling ball.

Other objects >

As well as the eight planets and 240 known moons, the solar system holds dwarf planets, asteroids, icy Kuiper Belt objects, meteoroids, comets, and dust. All these objects are held in orbit around the Sun by gravity.

> WHAT IS THE KUIPER BELT?

It is a region of the solar system that lies beyond Neptune. Thousands of relatively small, frozen objects orbit there.

PLUTO

Pluto was called a planet until 2006, when it was reclassified.

> WHAT IS AN ASTEROID?

Asteroids are the thousands of rocky lumps that circle around the Sun in a big band between Mars and Jupiter. Some venture outside this zone. Unlike the frozen Kuiper Belt objects, asteroids are mostly made of rock and metal. More than 5,000 asteroids have been identified so far.

> WHAT ARE DWARF PLANETS?

There are four dwarf planets currently known in the solar system. They are Pluto, Ceres, Makemake, and Eris. These bodies are large enough to be made rounded by their own gravity, but not large enough to have cleared the area around them of other bodies.

METEOR CRATER

Meteor Crater, in Arizona, was made by a meteorite 160 feet across.

NUCLEUS

At the heart of a comet is a nucleus of ice and rock, often shaped like a lumpy potato and just a few miles across.

WHAT IS A METEORITE?

Meteorites are lumps of rock from space big enough to penetrate Earth's atmosphere and reach the ground without burning up.

WHAT IS A COMET?

Comets are just dirty ice balls. Normally, they circle the outer solar system. But occasionally, one of them is drawn in toward the Sun. As it hurtles along, material from its surface is blown away from the Sun by the solar wind. We may see this tail in the night sky, shining in the sunlight until it swings out of sight.

HOW LONG IS A COMET'S TAIL?

It can be millions of miles long. If a comet's path crosses Earth's path, there may be meteor showers of debris.

METEORITE

More than 32,000 meteorites have been found on Earth. Some are as small as marbles.

Stars and galaxies

Birth of the universe

Scientists define the universe as absolutely everything that physically exists. But the universe has not always existed. It is believed that the universe was created by the big bang, when it started to grow from a tiny point that contained all matter and energy.

> WHAT WAS THE UNIVERSE LIKE AT THE BEGINNING?

The early universe was very small, but it contained all the matter and energy in the universe today. It was a dense and chaotic soup of tiny particles and forces. But this original universe lasted only a split second—just three trillionths of a trillionth of a trillionth of a second.

> WHAT WAS THERE BEFORE THE UNIVERSE?

No one knows. Some people think there was an unimaginable ocean, beyond space and time, of potential universes continually bursting into life or failing. Ours succeeded.

> CAN WE SEE THE BIG BANG?

Astronomers can see the galaxies still hurtling away from the big bang in all directions. They can also see the afterglow—low-level microwave radiation coming at us from all over the sky, called background radiation.

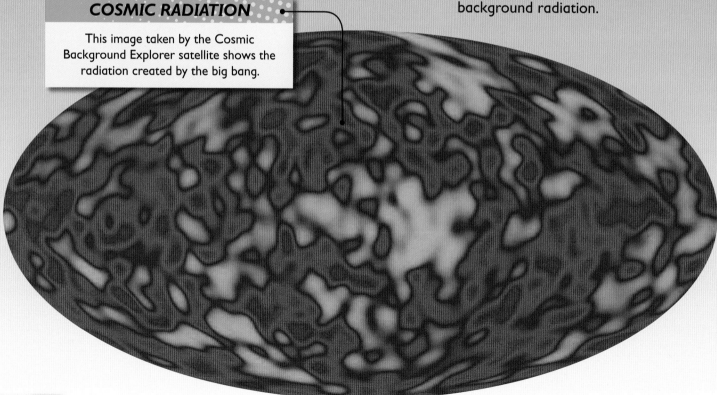

COSMIC RADIATION

This image taken by the Cosmic Background Explorer satellite shows the radiation created by the big bang.

YOUNG UNIVERSE

This artist's impression shows how the young universe may have looked as stars burst into being like fireworks.

NEW GALAXY

As it started to form, 12.7 billion years ago, our own galaxy may have looked like this.

TOP QUESTION

WHAT WAS THE BIG BANG?

In the beginning, all the universe was squeezed into an unimaginably small, hot, dense ball. The big bang was when this suddenly began to swell explosively, allowing first energy and matter, then atoms, gas clouds, and galaxies to form. The universe has been swelling ever since.

> ## HOW DO WE KNOW WHAT THE EARLY UNIVERSE WAS LIKE?

Machines called colliders and particle accelerators can recreate conditions in the early universe by using magnets to accelerate particles to astonishing speeds and then crashing them together.

> ## HOW HOT WAS THE BIG BANG?

As the universe grew from smaller than an atom to the size of a soccer ball, it cooled from infinity to eighteen billion billion billion°F.

Growing universe

The universe has continued to expand ever since the big bang. Scientists are not sure if it will carry on growing forever, beyond what we can possibly observe, or whether it will eventually come to a stop and end in a big crunch.

WHAT IS INFLATION?

Inflation was when dramatic expansion and cooling took place just a tiny fraction of a second after the big bang.

HOW LONG WILL THE UNIVERSE LAST?

It depends how much matter it contains. If there is more than the "critical density," gravity will put a brake on its expansion, and it may soon begin to contract again to end in a big crunch. If there is much less, it may go on expanding forever.

TOP QUESTION

HOW DID THE FIRST GALAXIES FORM?

They formed from lumps of clouds of hydrogen and helium, as concentrations within the clumps drew together. The youngest known galaxy (right) is just 500 million years old and typical of the galaxies of the early universe.

WHAT SHAPE IS THE UNIVERSE?

Scientists do not yet know—rather like early humankind had no way of knowing the shape of our own Earth. Perhaps the universe is flat, perhaps it is a curve, or perhaps even a sphere.

SPEEDING APART

All the galaxies are speeding apart from each other, much like raisins in a continuously raising loaf of bread.

> HOW DO WE KNOW THAT THE UNIVERSE IS GETTING BIGGER?

We can tell the universe is getting bigger because distant galaxies are speeding away from us. Yet the galaxies themselves are not moving—the space in between them is stretching.

> HOW OLD IS THE UNIVERSE?

We know that the universe is getting bigger at a certain rate by observing how fast distant galaxies are moving apart. By working out how long it took everything to expand to where it is now, we can work out that the universe may be about 13.7 billion years old.

DISTANT GALAXIES

As their light takes time to reach us, distant galaxies seen through a telescope are seen as they were millions of years ago.

Matter and particles >

Matter is simply anything that has mass and takes up space. All matter is made up of tiny particles, such as protons, neutrons, and electrons. Particles are the building blocks of the universe.

> WHAT IS THE UNIVERSE MADE FROM?

The stars and clouds in space are made almost 100 percent of hydrogen and helium, the lightest and simplest atoms, or elements. All the other elements are fairly rare. But some, such as carbon, oxygen, silicon, nitrogen, and iron, can form important concentrations, as in the rocky planets, such as Earth, where iron, oxygen, and magnesium are among the most common elements.

> HOW WERE ATOMS MADE?

Atoms of hydrogen and helium were made in the early days of the universe when quarks in the matter soup joined together. All other atoms were made as atoms were fused together by the intense heat and pressure inside stars.

ATOM

A cloud of particles called electrons surrounds the atom's nucleus.

> WHAT ARE QUARKS?

Quarks are tiny particles much smaller than atoms. They were among the first particles to form at the birth of the universe.

NUCLEUS

The nucleus, or center, of an atom is made of protons and neutrons, which are themselves made of quarks.

ATOM SMASHER

A particle accelerator propels particles at immense speeds to investigate their nature.

WHAT IS THE SMALLEST KNOWN PARTICLE?

The smallest particle inside the nucleus is the quark. It is less than 10^{-20} feet across, which means a line of ten billion billion of them would be less than a foot long.

➤ WHAT ARE PARTICLES?

Particles are the basic units of matter that make up everyday objects. There are hundreds of kinds of particles, but all, apart from the atom and molecule, are too small to see, even with the most powerful microscope.

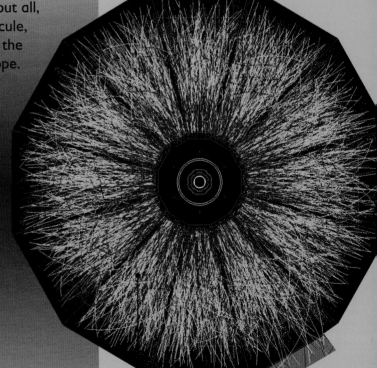

➤ WHAT IS ANTIMATTER?

Antimatter is the mirror image of ordinary matter. If matter and antimatter meet, they destroy each other. Fortunately, there is no antimatter on Earth.

SCATTERED ATOMS

The paths of subatomic particles, such as quarks, can be seen after colliding atoms at great speed.

The birth of stars >

Stars are gigantic glowing balls of gas, scattered throughout space. They burn for anything from a few million to tens of billions of years. The closest star to the Earth is our Sun.

> HOW ARE STARS BORN?

Stars are born when clumps of gas in space are drawn together by their own gravity, and the middle of the clump is squeezed so hard that temperatures reach 18 million°F, so a nuclear fusion reaction starts. The heat makes the star shine.

> WHERE ARE STARS BORN?

Stretched throughout space are vast clouds of dust and gas called nebulae. These clouds are 99 percent hydrogen and helium with tiny amounts of other gases and minute quantities of icy, cosmic dust. Stars are born in the biggest of these nebulae, which are called giant molecular clouds.

EAGLE NEBULA

Stars are being formed in the Eagle Nebula, which was photographed by the Hubble Space Telescope.

STAR BIRTH

New stars are seen glowing as bright spots.

> HOW CLOSE ARE THE STARS?

The nearest star, apart from the Sun, is around 25 trillion miles away. The stars are so distant that we can see them only as pinpoints of light in the night sky.

> CAN WE SEE NEBULAE FROM EARTH?

Some nebulae can be seen through telescopes because they shine as they reflect starlight. Others, called dark nebulae, are seen as inky black patches. A few, called glowing nebulae, glow as the gas within them is heated by nearby stars.

> HOW DOES A STAR BURN STEADILY?

In medium-size stars, such as our Sun, the heat generated in the core pushes gas out as hard as gravity pulls it in, so the star burns steadily for billions of years.

> WHICH IS THE CLOSEST NEBULA TO EARTH?

It is the Orion Nebula (below right), which is 1,500 light-years, or 9 thousand million million miles, away.

NEBULAE

Nebulae occur in many different shapes. From left to right are the Cone, Horsehead, and Orion Nebulae.

Shining stars →

Many stars are visible in the night sky, when they are not outshone by the Sun. Humankind has studied the stars for millennia, with the oldest known star chart dating back 3,500 years. Today, the position of the stars is still used for navigation.

❯ WHAT ARE CONSTELLATIONS?

Constellations are small patterns of stars in the sky, each with its own name. They are often named after the object or figure that they resemble, such as a lion or cross. Different cultures identify different constellations. The stars in a constellation may not be very close to each other in reality—they only appear to be close when viewed from Earth.

ORION

The constellation of Orion is one of the brightest in the night sky.

❯ WHERE IS THE POLE STAR?

The Pole Star is a bright star that lies directly over the North Pole. With a long camera exposure, the stars seem to rotate around the Pole Star as the Earth turns (above).

TOP QUESTION ?

WHERE IS THE HUNTER?

The constellation of Orion looks like a hunter holding a sword. The hunter's head, shoulders, three-star belt, legs, and sword can be seen.

HOW HOT IS A STAR?

The surface temperature of the coolest stars is below 6,300°F; that of the hottest, brightest stars is over 70,000°F.

WHAT COLORS ARE STARS?

It depends how hot they are. The color of medium-size stars varies along a band on a graph called the main sequence—from hot and bright blue-white stars to cool and dim red stars.

WHAT MAKES STARS GLOW?

Stars glow because the enormous pressure deep inside generates nuclear fusion reactions in which hydrogen atoms are fused together, releasing huge quantities of energy.

RED STAR

Older stars are often cooler and dimmer and take on a reddish glow.

WHITE STARS

Young stars often burn hot and bright and can be seen as blue-white lights in the night sky.

Star giants and dwarfs ›

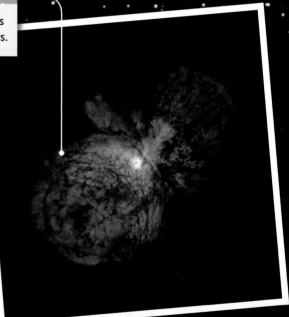

VARIABLE STAR

The star Eta Carinae brightens and dims over a period of years.

Stars are classified depending on their size and how brightly they are burning. Large stars burn their fuel very fast and are short-lived. Small stars burn their fuel slowly and can last for billions of years.

› HOW MANY STARS ARE THERE?

It is hard to know how many stars there are in the universe—most are much too far away to see. But astronomers guess there are about 200 billion billion.

› WHAT IS A RED DWARF?

A red dwarf is a small and fairly cool star with a mass less than 40 percent that of the Sun. The majority of stars are believed to be red dwarfs.

› WHICH STARS THROB?

The light from variable stars flares up and down. "Cepheid" stars are big old stars that pulsate over a few days or a few weeks. "RR Lyrae" variables are old yellow stars that vary over a few hours.

PERSEUS

The constellation of Perseus contains a variable star called Algol. Its brightest star is a supergiant called Mirfak.

STAR SIZES

The size of stars is measured in solar masses—or how many times the size of our Sun they are.

WHAT MAKES STARS TWINKLE?

Stars twinkle because Earth's atmosphere is never still, and starlight twinkles as the air wavers. Light from the nearby planets is not distorted as much, so they don't twinkle.

WHICH IS THE BIGGEST STAR?

The biggest stars are the supergiants. Antares is 700 times as big as the Sun. There may be a star in the Epsilon system in the constellation of Auriga that is 1.8 billion miles across—4,000 times bigger than the Sun.

TOP QUESTION ?

WHAT IS A RED GIANT?

It is a huge, cool star, near the end of its life cycle, when the fuel begins to exhaust and the star expands to about fifty times its normal size.

Red dwarf
0.4 solar masses

Blue-white giant
150 solar masses

Sun
1 solar mass

Red giant
5 solar masses

The death of stars >

Stars make energy by turning hydrogen into helium. When the hydrogen is used up, they then use any other nuclear energy. When a star's supplies of energy are all gone, it dies.

> HOW OLD ARE STARS?

Stars are dying and being born all the time. Big, bright stars live for only 10 million years. Medium-size stars like our Sun live for 10 billion years.

> WHAT HAPPENS WHEN STARS DIE?

When a star has used up all its energy, it either blows up, shrinks, turns cold, or becomes a black hole. Just how long it takes to reach this point depends on the size of the star. The biggest stars have masses of nuclear fuel, but live fast and die young. The smallest stars have little nuclear fuel, but live slow and long. A star twice as big as the Sun lives a tenth as long.

❯ HOW WILL OUR SUN DIE?

The Sun will exhaust its supply of hydrogen fuel in about 4 billion years. Its core will crash inward and become hot enough to ignite its helium atoms. The Sun will now swell up to become a red giant. The outer layers will drift off, making a planetary nebula, leaving behind the core of the Sun. This will gradually cool off.

❯ WHAT IS A PULSAR?

Pulsars are stars that flash out intense radio pulses every ten seconds or less as they spin rapidly. They are thought to be very dense dying stars called neutron stars.

❯ WHAT IS A WHITE DWARF?

White dwarfs are the small dense stars formed when the outer layers of a star like the Sun are blown off during the last parts of the red giant stage.

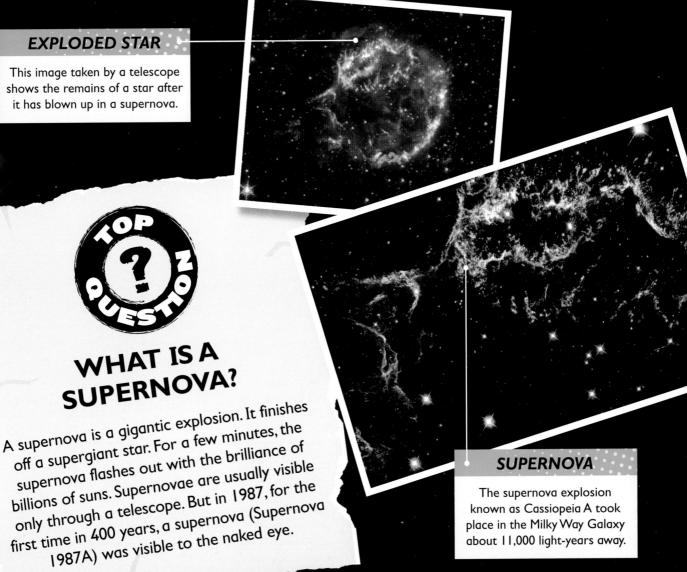

EXPLODED STAR

This image taken by a telescope shows the remains of a star after it has blown up in a supernova.

TOP ? QUESTION

WHAT IS A SUPERNOVA?

A supernova is a gigantic explosion. It finishes off a supergiant star. For a few minutes, the supernova flashes out with the brilliance of billions of suns. Supernovae are usually visible only through a telescope. But in 1987, for the first time in 400 years, a supernova (Supernova 1987A) was visible to the naked eye.

SUPERNOVA

The supernova explosion known as Cassiopeia A took place in the Milky Way Galaxy about 11,000 light-years away.

Star groups >

In addition to single stars, stars exist in multistar groups that orbit around each other. Larger groups called star clusters also occur. Stars are not spread uniformly across the universe. They are normally grouped in galaxies.

BINARY STARS
The star Sirius A has a small companion called Sirius B.

> WHAT ARE CLUSTERS?

Stars are rarely entirely alone within a galaxy. Many are concentrated in groups called clusters. Globular clusters are big and round. Galactic clusters are small and formless.

> WHAT ARE DOUBLE STARS?

Our Sun is alone in space, but many stars have one or more nearby companions. Double stars are called binaries.

WHAT ARE THE PLEIADES?

The Pleiades are a group of 400 stars, 7 of which are visible to the naked eye, that formed in the same cloud of dust and gas. The stars are held loosely together by gravity.

THE MILKY WAY

Our Galaxy looks like a milky band in the night sky, but if we could view it from above, we would see that the Milky Way is a giant spiral.

❯ WHAT IS A GALAXY?

Our Sun is just one of 200 billion stars arranged in a shape like a fried egg, 100,000 light-years across. This star group is our Galaxy, which is just one of billions of galaxies scattered throughout space.

❯ WHAT IS THE MILKY WAY?

Our Galaxy is called the Milky Way. This is because it can be seen stretching across the night sky in a blotchy white band. This is our edge-on view of the Galaxy. Since our own Galaxy was the first one that astronomers knew about, they came up with the word "galaxy," which comes from the Greek word for "milky."

❯ WHAT IS THE BIGGEST THING IN THE UNIVERSE?

The biggest structure in the universe is the Great Wall—a great sheet of galaxies 500 million light- years long and 16 million light-years thick.

Types of galaxies →

A galaxy is a massive system of stars, gas, and dust, held together by gravity. Galaxies are classified by their shape, which may be spiral, elliptical, or irregular. Sometimes, galaxies can merge or collide with each other.

› WHAT ARE SPIRAL GALAXIES?

Spiral galaxies are spinning pinwheel spirals like our Milky Way. Barred spiral galaxies have a bar crossing the center with arms trailing from it.

› WHAT ARE IRREGULAR GALAXIES?

Irregular galaxies are galaxies that have no particular shape at all.

› WHERE IS EARTH?

Earth is just over halfway out along one of the spiral arms of the Milky Way Galaxy, about 30,000 light-years from the center. The Galaxy is whirling rapidly, sweeping us around at 60,000 miles an hour.

SPIRAL GALAXY

The neat spiral galaxy named M81 has perfect arms spiraling into its center.

IRREGULAR GALAXY

Most irregular galaxies were once spiral or elliptical, but have been pulled apart by gravity.

ELLIPTICAL GALAXY

The elliptical galaxy known as Fornax A is at the edge of a cluster of galaxies known as the Fornax Cluster.

> WHAT ARE ELLIPTICAL GALAXIES?

Elliptical galaxies are shaped like rugby balls. There is no gas and dust remaining in an elliptical galaxy, so no new stars can form.

> ARE GALAXIES IN GROUPS?

Yes! Most galaxies are in clusters, which can form larger groups called superclusters. And superclusters are grouped into sheets and threadlike filaments, which surround huge voids in the universe.

> HOW MANY GALAXIES ARE THERE?

There are currently estimated to be about 125 billion galaxies in the universe, but there may be many, many more than this.

Black holes >

A black hole is a region that has such an immense gravitational pull that it sucks space into a "hole" like a funnel. Not even light can escape the pull of a black hole, which is why it is called "black." The hole's interior cannot be seen.

> HOW IS A BLACK HOLE FORMED?

When a large star becomes a supernova, the center of the star is violently compressed by the shock of the explosion. As it compresses, it becomes denser and denser and its gravity becomes more and more powerful—until it shrinks to a single tiny point of infinite density called a singularity. The singularity sucks space into a black hole.

> HOW CAN WE SEE A BLACK HOLE?

The black hole contains so much matter in such a small space that its gravitational pull even drags in light. We may be able to see a black hole from the powerful radiation emitted by stars being ripped to shreds as they are sucked in. A giant black hole may exist at the center of our Galaxy.

HOLE AT THE CENTER

It is believed that the galaxy Centaurus A, like many galaxies, has a black hole at its center.

> WHAT HAPPENS INSIDE A BLACK HOLE?

Nothing that goes into a black hole comes out. Everything is torn apart by the immense gravity.

> HOW MANY BLACK HOLES ARE THERE?

No one really knows. Because they trap light, they are hard to see. But there may be as many as 100 million black holes in the Milky Way.

> HOW BIG IS A BLACK HOLE?

The singularity at the heart of a black hole is infinitely small. The size of the black hole is usually taken to be the size of the volume of space from which light cannot escape. The black hole at the heart of our Galaxy may be the size of the solar system.

WHAT IS GRAVITY?

Gravity is the mutual attraction between every part of matter in the universe. The more matter there is, and the closer it is, the stronger the attraction. A big planet pulls much more than a small one, or one that is far away. The Sun is so big, it makes its pull felt over millions of miles.

BLACK HOLE

This artist's impression shows what a black hole at the center of a galaxy might look like.

Distances in the universe >

Spacecraft have never traveled beyond our solar system, so we have no way of directly measuring distances in the wider universe. Astronomers can perform complicated calculations to work out the distances of faraway stars.

> WHAT IS A LIGHT-YEAR?

A light-year is 5,875,000,000,000 miles. This is the distance light can travel in a year, at its constant rate of 185,000 miles per second.

> HOW FAR IS IT TO THE NEAREST STAR?

The nearest star is Proxima Centauri, which is 4.3 light-years away, or 25 trillion miles.

CLOSEST STAR

Since Proxima Centauri is so close to us, its diameter can be calculated as about an eighth of the Sun's.

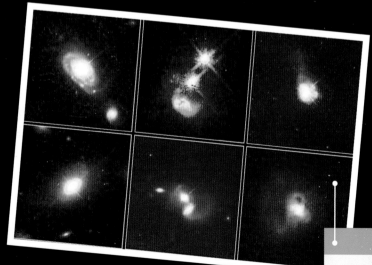

> WHAT ARE STANDARD CANDLES?

When measuring the distance to middle-distance stars, astronomers compare the star's brightness to stars that they know, or "standard candles." The dimmer the star looks in comparison, the farther away it is.

QUASARS

The farthest objects we can see with telescopes are quasars, which may be 13 billion light years away. Quasars probably surround black holes.

WHAT IS THE FARTHEST OBJECT WE CAN SEE?

The farthest object visible with the naked eye is the Andromeda Galaxy, which is about 2.5 million light-years away. It is visible as a smudge in the night sky. A better view is gained with binoculars or a telescope.

WHAT IS A PARSEC?

A parsec is 3.26 light-years. Parsecs are parallax distances—distances worked out geometrically from slight shifts of a star's apparent position as Earth moves around the Sun.

WHAT IS RED SHIFT?

When a galaxy is moving away from us, the waves of light become stretched out— that is, they become redder. The greater this red shift, the faster the galaxy is moving.

ANDROMEDA

The Andromeda Galaxy is the closest large galaxy to the Milky Way. Both galaxies are part of the Local Group of galaxies.

STELLAR DISK

It is estimated that the Andromeda Galaxy's disk of stars may be 220,000 light-years across.

Life in the universe

As far as we know, Earth is the only planet in the universe on which life exists. But perhaps in other galaxies there are planets in orbit around a star, like the Earth orbits the Sun. Could there be life on such planets?

HOW DID LIFE BEGIN?

Scientific experiments in the 1950s showed how lightning flashes might create amino acids, the basic chemicals of life, from the waters and gases of the early Earth. But no one knows how these chemicals were able to make copies of themselves. This is the key to life, which remains a mystery.

WHAT IS LIFE MADE OF?

Life is based on compounds of the element carbon, known as organic chemicals. Carbon compounds called amino acids link up to form proteins, and proteins form the chemicals that build and maintain living cells.

WHAT IS SETI?

SETI is the Search for Extra-Terrestrial Intelligence project, designed to continually scan radio signals from space and pick up any signs of intelligence. It looks for signals that have a pattern, but are not completely regular, like those from pulsating stars.

SEARCHING FOR LIFE

These vast radio telescopes in New Mexico constantly scan the universe for radio waves.

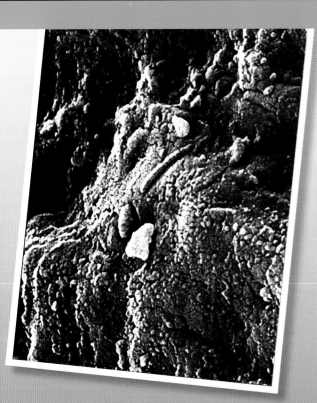

➤ WHERE DID THE MATERIALS OF LIFE COME FROM?

It used to be thought that organic chemicals all originated on Earth, but many complicated organic compounds, including amino acids, have been detected in molecular clouds.

➤ HOW DO WE LOOK FOR EXTRATERRESTRIAL LIFE?

Since possible fossils of microscopic life were seen in a Martian meteorite found on Earth in 1996 (above), scientists have hunted for other signs of organisms in rocks from space.

MARS ROVER

Robotic probes are currently looking for signs that there was once life on Mars. Today, the planet is uninhabitable.

TOP ? QUESTION

IS THERE LIFE ON OTHER PLANETS?

In such a large universe, there are probably many planets, like Earth, suitable for life. But no one knows if life arose on Earth by a unique chance or whether it is likely to happen again given the right conditions.

Elements and substances

Atoms and particles >

Atoms are what every substance is made of. They are the smallest part of any substance. Yet atoms are mostly composed of empty space—and dotted with even tinier clouds of energy called subatomic particles.

> WHAT IS THE NUCLEUS?

Most of an atom is empty space, but at its center is a tiny area called the nucleus. This contains two kinds of nuclear particle—neutrons with no electrical charge, and protons with a positive electrical charge. A hydrogen atom contains no neutrons and one proton.

ELECTRON

A helium atom has two electrons. Their negative charge balances the positive charge of the protons.

> HOW BIG ARE ATOMS?

Atoms are about a ten-millionth of a millimeter across and weigh a hundred trillionths of a trillionth of a gram. The smallest atom is hydrogen; the most massive is ununoctium.

HELIUM ATOM

A helium atom contains two protons and two neutrons in its nucleus. It is the second smallest atom.

➤ WHAT IS THE SMALLEST PARTICLE?

No one is sure. Atoms are made of protons, neutrons, and electrons. In turn, these are made of even tinier particles—quarks and leptons. Scientists know about more than 200 kinds of subatomic particles so far. But one day we might discover even smaller particles.

➤ WHAT ARE ELECTRONS?

Electrons are the negatively electrically charged particles that whiz around inside an atom. They were discovered by the English physicist J. J. Thomson (1856–1940) in 1897 during some experiments with cathode-ray tubes.

CATHODE-RAY TUBE

A stream of electrons is fired into a vacuum, or totally empty, tube.

➤ CAN ATOMS JOIN TOGETHER?

Yes! Electrons are held to the nucleus by electrical attraction, because they have an opposite electrical charge to the protons in the nucleus. But electrons can also be drawn to the nuclei of other atoms. This is when bonding takes place.

WHIZZING

Electrons whirl around inside the atom.

TOP ? QUESTION

WHO FIRST SPLIT THE ATOM?

In 1919, the physicist Ernest Rutherford (right) managed to break down nitrogen atoms into hydrogen and oxygen. In 1932, his students John Cockcroft and Ernest Walton managed to split the nucleus of an atom by firing protons at it.

Elements →

An element is a substance that cannot be split up into other substances. Water is not an element because it can be split into the gases oxygen and hydrogen. Oxygen and hydrogen are elements because they cannot be split.

❯ WHAT IS ATOMIC NUMBER?

Every element has its own atomic number. This is the number of protons in its nucleus, which is balanced by the same number of electrons. Hydrogen, with one proton, is number 1.

Hydrogen

❯ WHAT ARE ELECTRON SHELLS?

Electrons behave as if they are stacked around the nucleus at different levels, like the layers of an onion. These levels are called shells and there is room for a particular number of electrons in each shell. The number of electrons in the outer shell determines how the atom will react with other atoms. Carbon has four electrons in its outer shell and room for four more, so carbon atoms link very readily with other atoms.

❯ WHAT IS ATOMIC MASS?

Atomic mass is the "weight" of one whole atom of a substance, which is of course very tiny! It includes both protons and neutrons.

Oxygen

WATER MOLECULE

A molecule of water is composed of two hydrogen atoms bonded to one oxygen atom by electrons.

SULFUR

The element sulfur has an atomic number of 16.

TOP QUESTION ?

WHAT IS THE LIGHTEST ELEMENT?

The lightest element is hydrogen. It has just one proton in its nucleus and has an atomic mass of just one. Hydrogen is the most common element in the universe.

HYDROGEN AIRSHIP

Since hydrogen is lighter than air, it was once used in airships. However, it is also very flammable.

Hydrogen

➤ WHAT IS A MOLECULE?

Very often, atoms join up with other atoms—either of the same kind, or with other kinds to form chemical compounds. A molecule is the smallest part of a substance that can exist on its own.

➤ HOW MANY ELEMENTS ARE THERE?

New elements are sometimes discovered, but the total number identified so far is 118.

The periodic table

Elements can be ordered into a chart called the periodic table. Columns are called groups; rows are called periods. Elements in a group have the same number of electrons in the outer shell of their atoms and similar properties—such as being hard and shiny.

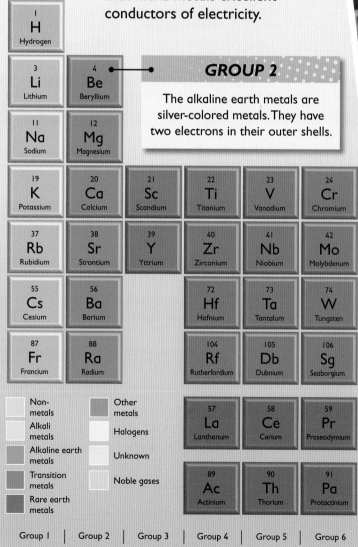

> WHAT ARE THE TRANSITION METALS?

Transition metals are the metals in the middle of the periodic table, such as gold, chromium, and silver (left). They are usually shiny and tough, but easily shaped.

> WHAT ARE NOBLE GASES?

The noble gases are in the farthest right-hand column of the periodic table. These gases do not readily react with other elements. But krypton, radon, and xenon do combine with fluorine and oxygen to form compounds.

> WHY ARE SOME ELEMENTS REACTIVE?

Elements are reactive if they readily gain or lose electrons. Elements on the left of the periodic table, called metals, lose electrons very easily. The farther left they are, the more reactive they are.

> WHAT IS A METAL?

A metal is hard, dense, and shiny, and goes "ping" when you strike it with another metal. It also conducts, or transfers, electricity and heat well. Chemists define a metal as an electropositive element, which means that metals easily lose negatively charged electrons. It is these lost, "free" electrons that make metals excellent conductors of electricity.

GROUP 2

The alkaline earth metals are silver-colored metals. They have two electrons in their outer shells.

Non-metals
Alkali metals
Alkaline earth metals
Transition metals
Rare earth metals
Other metals
Halogens
Unknown
Noble gases

Group 1 | Group 2 | Group 3 | Group 4 | Group 5 | Group 6

WHO DISCOVERED RADIUM?

The Polish-French physicist Marie Curie (1867–1934; left) was the first woman to win not one, but two, Nobel prizes. The first, in 1903, was for her part in the discovery of radioactivity, and the second, in 1911, for her discovery of the elements polonium (group 16 in the periodic table) and radium (group 2).

WHAT ARE LANTHANIDES?

The lanthanides are a group of 15 elements one row above the bottom of the table. They take their name from lanthanum. They are all shiny, silvery metals, and often occur naturally together. They all have two or three electrons in their outer shells.

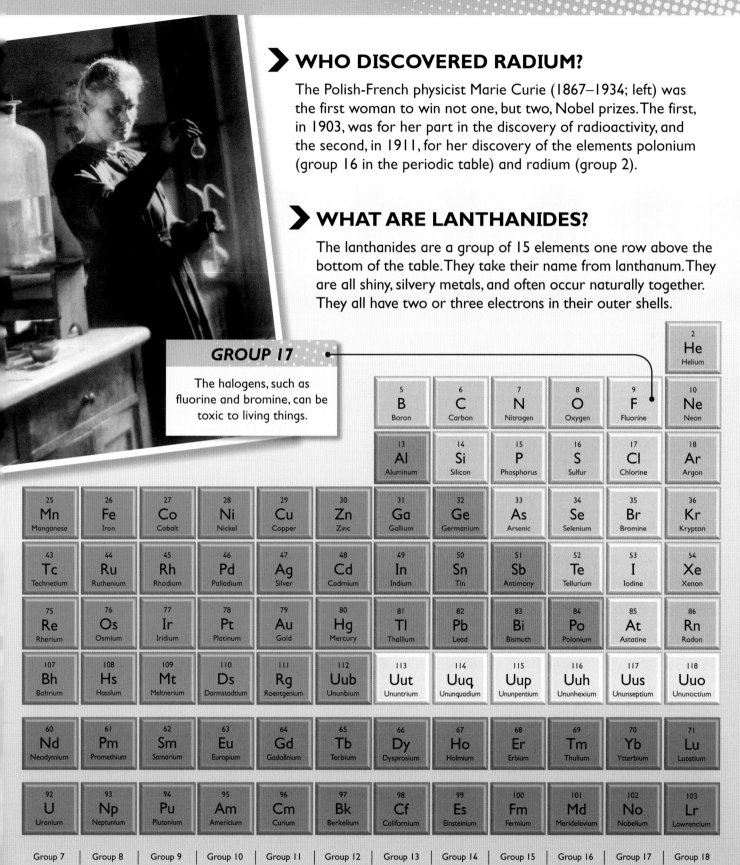

GROUP 17

The halogens, such as fluorine and bromine, can be toxic to living things.

2 He Helium

5 B Boron	6 C Carbon	7 N Nitrogen	8 O Oxygen	9 F Fluorine	10 Ne Neon
13 Al Aluminum	14 Si Silicon	15 P Phosphorus	16 S Sulfur	17 Cl Chlorine	18 Ar Argon

25 Mn Manganese	26 Fe Iron	27 Co Cobalt	28 Ni Nickel	29 Cu Copper	30 Zn Zinc	31 Ga Gallium	32 Ge Germanium	33 As Arsenic	34 Se Selenium	35 Br Bromine	36 Kr Krypton
43 Tc Technetium	44 Ru Ruthenium	45 Rh Rhodium	46 Pd Palladium	47 Ag Silver	48 Cd Cadmium	49 In Indium	50 Sn Tin	51 Sb Antimony	52 Te Tellurium	53 I Iodine	54 Xe Xenon
75 Re Rherium	76 Os Osmium	77 Ir Iridium	78 Pt Platinum	79 Au Gold	80 Hg Mercury	81 Tl Thallium	82 Pb Lead	83 Bi Bismuth	84 Po Polonium	85 At Astatine	86 Rn Radon
107 Bh Bohrium	108 Hs Hasslum	109 Mt Meltnerium	110 Ds Darmstadtium	111 Rg Roentgenium	112 Uub Ununbium	113 Uut Ununtrium	114 Uuq Ununquadium	115 Uup Ununpentium	116 Uuh Ununhexium	117 Uus Ununseptium	118 Uuo Ununoctium

60 Nd Neodymium	61 Pm Promethium	62 Sm Samarium	63 Eu Europium	64 Gd Gadollnium	65 Tb Terbium	66 Dy Dysprosium	67 Ho Holmium	68 Er Erbium	69 Tm Thulium	70 Yb Ytterbium	71 Lu Lutetium
92 U Uranium	93 Np Neptunium	94 Pu Plutonium	95 Am Americium	96 Cm Curium	97 Bk Berkelium	98 Cf Californium	99 Es Einsteinium	100 Fm Fermium	101 Md Meridelevium	102 No Nobelium	103 Lr Lawrencium

Group 7	Group 8	Group 9	Group 10	Group 11	Group 12	Group 13	Group 14	Group 15	Group 16	Group 17	Group 18

Solids and liquids

Substances can be solid, liquid, or gas. These are the different states of matter. Substances move from one state to another when they are heated or cooled, boosting or reducing the energy of their particles.

❯ WHAT ARE SOLIDS?

In solids, particles are locked together, so solids have a definite shape and volume. In liquids, particles move around a little, so liquids can flow into any shape, while their volume stays the same. In gases, particles zoom around all over the place, so gases spread out to fill containers of any size or shape.

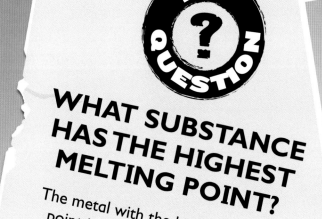

TOP QUESTION ?

WHAT SUBSTANCE HAS THE HIGHEST MELTING POINT?

The metal with the highest melting point is tungsten, which melts at 6,170°F. But the highest known melting point of any substance belongs to carbon, which melts at 6,381°F.

ICE, WATER, AND STEAM

At this hot spring in Iceland, water is in three states: solid, liquid, and gas.

❯ WHAT IS SNOW?

Snow is composed of small ice particles. The particles are formed when water droplets in a cloud get so cold they freeze. The ice particles start to stick together, forming snowflakes. Once the flakes are heavy enough, they fall.

> WHEN DO THINGS FREEZE?

Things freeze from liquid to solid when they reach the freezing point. Most substances get smaller when they freeze as the particles pack closer together. But water gets bigger as it turns to ice.

• MOLTEN IRON

At over 2,795°F, iron is liquid and can be poured.

> WHICH SUBSTANCE HAS THE LOWEST FREEZING POINT?

Mercury has the lowest freezing point of any metal, at -38°F. Helium has the lowest freezing point of all substances, at -452°F, which is less than 8° above absolute zero.

> WHEN DO THINGS MELT?

Things melt from solid to liquid on reaching a temperature called the melting point. Each substance has its own melting point. Water's is 32°F; lead's is 621.5°F.

ICE AND WATER

When ice cubes are put into water, heat from the water makes the molecules in the ice move faster and faster until they break free of the solid—and the cubes melt.

Gases >

A gas is one of the states of matter. Gas has no definite shape or volume. Its particles are in random motion. Gases can expand and contract, depending on pressure and temperature. They will grow to fill a container of any size.

> WHAT HAPPENS IN EVAPORATION AND CONDENSATION?

Evaporation happens when a liquid is warmed up and changes to a vapor. Particles at the liquid's surface vibrate so fast that they escape altogether. Condensation happens when a vapor is cooled down and becomes liquid. Evaporation and condensation take place not only at boiling point but also at much cooler temperatures.

> WHAT IS PLASMA?

A plasma is the fourth state of matter. It occurs only when a gas becomes so hot its atoms and molecules collide and electrons are ripped free. This happens inside the Sun, other stars, and lightning, and in gas neon tubes. Plasma displays, in which the plasma emits light, are used for many modern television screens.

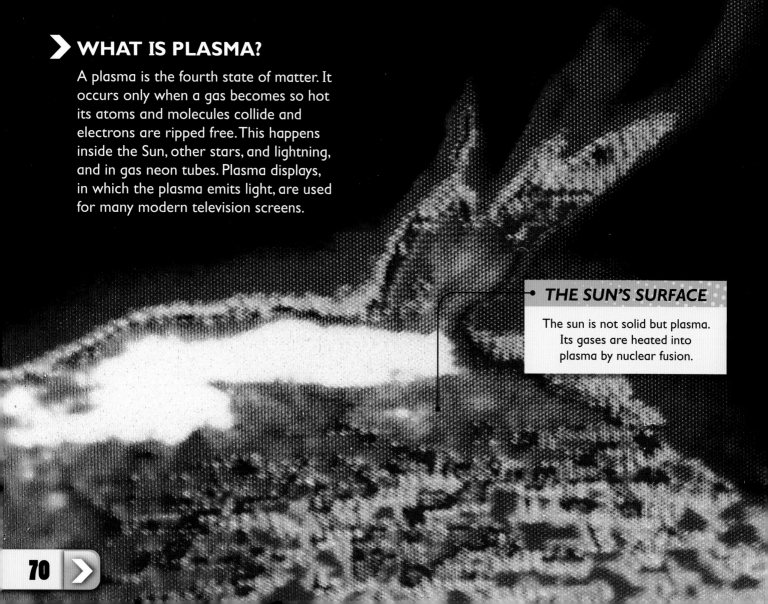

THE SUN'S SURFACE

The sun is not solid but plasma. Its gases are heated into plasma by nuclear fusion.

❯ WHEN DO THINGS BOIL?

Things boil from liquid to gas when they reach boiling point, which is the maximum temperature a liquid can reach. For water, this is 212°F.

Pressure is the amount of force pressing on something. Air pressure is the force with which air presses. The force comes from the bombardment of the moving air particles.

• BAROMETER

A barometer measures air pressure, which rises and falls depending on the weather.

❯ HOW DOES PRESSURE CHANGE?

If you squeeze a gas into half the space, the pressure doubles (as long as the temperature stays the same). This is Boyle's Law. If you warm up a gas, the pressure rises in proportion (as long as you keep it the same volume). This is the Pressure Law.

❯ WHAT ARE CLOUDS?

Clouds form when warm air is heated by the Sun and rises. As it rises, the warm air cools, eventually becoming cold enough for the water vapor it contains to condense into water droplets, which we can see as clouds.

Mixing chemicals >

The elements do not always exist alone. Often, elements react chemically with each other, forming compounds of two or more elements joined together. Elements may also dissolve in, or mix with, other elements without becoming joined as a compound.

> WHAT ARE COMPOUNDS?

They are substances made from two or more elements joined together. Every molecule in a compound is the same combination of atoms. Sodium chloride, for instance, is one atom of sodium joined to one of chlorine. Compounds have different properties from the elements that make them up. Sodium, for instance, spits when put in water; chlorine is a gas. Yet sodium chloride is table salt!

> HOW DO CHEMICALS REACT?

When substances react chemically, their atoms, ions, and molecules interact to form new combinations, separating elements from compounds or joining them together to form different compounds. Nearly all chemical reactions involve a change in energy, usually heat, as the bonds between particles are broken and formed.

SUGAR

Sugar is a compound of the elements carbon, hydrogen, and oxygen.

SALT DEPOSITS

The Dead Sea is the world's saltiest body of water. In the shallows, the water evaporates in the sunshine, leaving salt deposits.

➤ WHAT IS A MIXTURE?

Mixtures are substances that contain several chemical elements or compounds mixed together but not chemically joined. The chemicals intermingle but do not react with each other, and with the right technique can often be separated.

➤ WHAT IS AN ION?

An ion is an atom that has either lost one or a few electrons, making it positively charged (cation), or gained a few, making it negatively charged (anion). Ions usually form when substances dissolve in a liquid.

TOP QUESTION

HOW DO THINGS DISSOLVE?

When solids dissolve in liquid, it may look as if the solid disappears. Its atoms, ions, or molecules are, in fact, still intact—but are separated and evenly dispersed throughout the liquid.

DISSOLVING INK

When dropped in water, ink disperses until the water is evenly colored.

➤ WHAT IS THE SEA MADE OF?

The sea is water with oxygen, carbon dioxide, nitrogen, and various salts dissolved in it. The most abundant salt is common salt (sodium chloride). Others include Epsom salt (magnesium sulfate), magnesium chloride, potassium chloride, potassium bromide, and potassium iodide.

Chemical reactions →

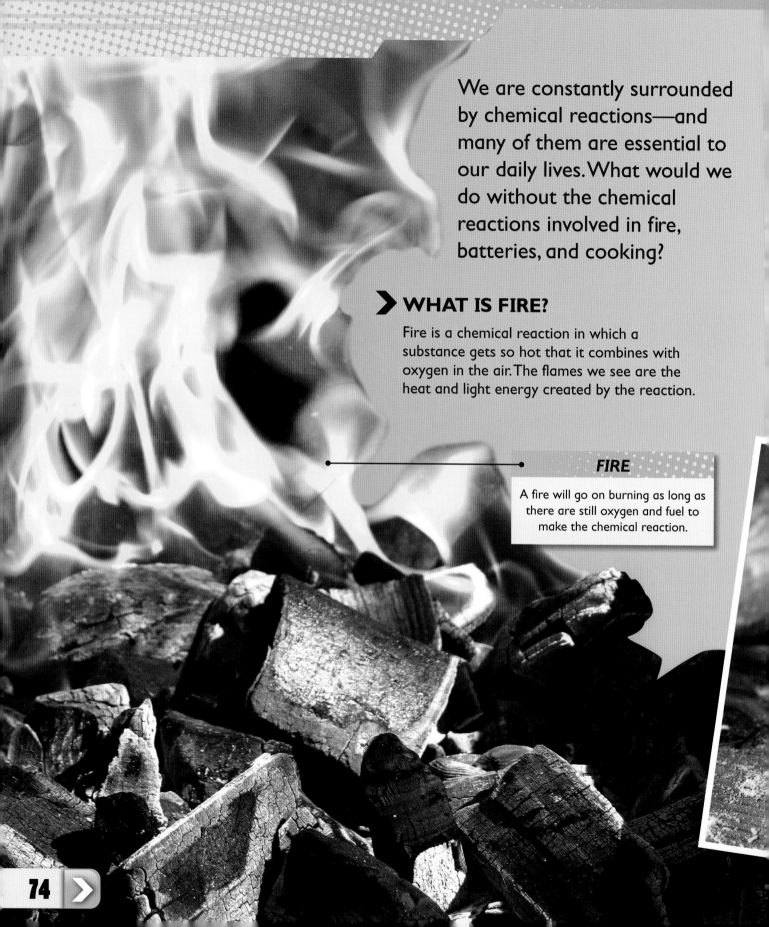

We are constantly surrounded by chemical reactions—and many of them are essential to our daily lives. What would we do without the chemical reactions involved in fire, batteries, and cooking?

❯ WHAT IS FIRE?

Fire is a chemical reaction in which a substance gets so hot that it combines with oxygen in the air. The flames we see are the heat and light energy created by the reaction.

FIRE

A fire will go on burning as long as there are still oxygen and fuel to make the chemical reaction.

➤ WHAT IS ELECTROLYSIS?

Electrolysis is a means of separating compounds by passing an electric current through them. It makes positive ions move to the negative terminal and negative ions to the positive. For example, electrolysis can make hydrogen out of water.

➤ WHAT IS A CHEMICAL FORMULA?

A chemical formula is a shorthand way of describing an atom, an ion, or a molecule. Initial letters (sometimes plus an extra letter) usually identify the atom or ion; a little number indicates how many atoms are involved. The formula for water is H_2O, because each molecule consists of two hydrogen atoms and one oxygen atom.

AIR COMPOSITION

The air in the earth's atmosphere is a mixture of different gases.

➤ IS AIR A COMPOUND?

No. Air is a mixture of elements and compounds but not a compound itself. Air contains 78 percent nitrogen and 21 percent oxygen with traces of argon, carbon dioxide, helium, neon, krypton, xenon, and radon.

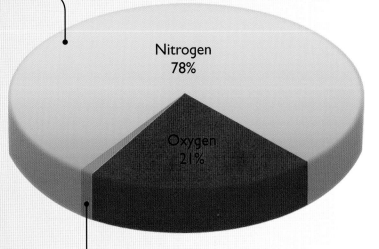

Nitrogen
78%

Oxygen
21%

Other gases less than 1%

➤ HOW DOES BREAD RISE?

Bakers add yeast, a type of fungus, to dough before they put it in the oven. When it is heated, yeast reacts with the sugar in the dough to make carbon dioxide. This gas forms pockets in the bread, making it rise.

BAKING BREAD

When dough is heated, a chemical reaction takes place between yeast and sugar.

➤ HOW DO BATTERIES WORK?

Batteries create electric currents from the reaction between two chemicals, one forming a positive electrode, or conductor of electricity, and the other a negative. The reaction creates an excess of electrons on the negative electrode, producing a current.

Radioactivity ➤

Radioactivity is when the nucleus of an atom is unstable and breaks down, emitting radiation in the form of alpha, beta, and gamma rays. These high-energy rays can be dangerous in large doses, causing burns and an increased risk of cancer.

➤ WHAT CAUSES RADIOACTIVITY?

The atoms of an element may come in several different forms, or isotopes. Each form has a different number of neutrons in the nucleus, indicated in the name, as in carbon-12 and carbon-14. The nuclei of some of these isotopes—the ones scientists call radioisotopes—are unstable, and they decay (break up), releasing radiation.

➤ WHAT IS HALF-LIFE?

No one can predict when an atomic nucleus will decay. But scientists can predict how long it will take for half the atoms in a quantity of a radioactive element to decay. This is its half-life. Francium-223 has a half-life of 22 minutes. Uranium-238 has a half-life of 4.5 billion years.

➤ WHICH ELEMENTS ARE VERY RADIOACTIVE?

The actinides are a group of 15 elements at the bottom of the periodic table that take their name from actinium. They include plutonium and uranium, and are radioactive.

HIGH LEVELS

Counters are used to detect dangerous radiation levels.

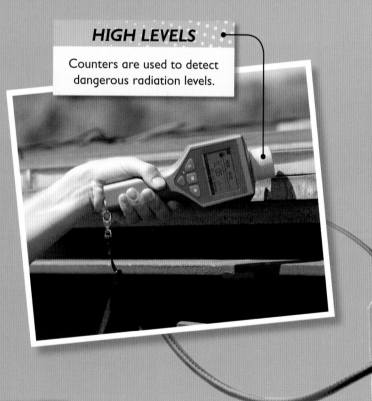

GEIGER COUNTER

A Geiger counter measures radioactivity by detecting alpha, beta, and gamma rays.

WHAT IS THE TURIN SHROUD?

The Turin Shroud (seen in a false-color image below) is a cloth that many Christians believe bears the imprint of Christ's face after Crucifixion. Carbon dating has been carried out to determine if the cloth is the right age for this to be true, but the results showed that the cloth is not old enough.

➤ WHAT IS URANIUM?

Uranium is a radioactive metallic element. It can have between 141 and 146 neutrons in its nucleus. Uranium is mined from uranium-bearing minerals, such as cuprosklodowskite (above).

➤ HOW CAN RADIOACTIVITY BE USED TO INDICATE AGE?

Radioactive decay happens at a steady rate. So by measuring how much of a substance has decayed radioactively, you can tell its age. With once-living things, the best radioactive isotope to measure is carbon-14. This is called carbon dating.

Nuclear power

The energy that binds together an atomic nucleus is enormous, even though the nucleus is tiny. By harnessing this energy, nuclear power stations can generate huge amounts of power with just a few tons of nuclear fuel.

POWER STATION

Cooling towers release waste steam into the air.

❶ FISSION

A nucleus splits when it is hit by a neutron.

❯ WHAT IS NUCLEAR FISSION?

Nuclear fission releases nuclear energy by splitting big atomic nuclei, usually those of uranium. Neutrons are fired at the nuclei. As the neutrons smash into the nuclei, they split off more neutrons, which bombard other nuclei, setting off a chain reaction.

❷ COLLISION

❯ HOW DO NUCLEAR POWER STATIONS WORK?

A nuclear reactor houses fuel rods made from uranium dioxide. A nuclear fission chain reaction is set up in the fuel rods. The resulting energy is used to heat water, which produces steam to drive the turbines, or wheels, that generate electricity.

❸ CHAIN REACTION

Additional collisions result in smaller and smaller nuclei.

NEUTRON

The collisions split off more neutrons.

❯ HOW MUCH ELECTRICITY IS MADE BY NUCLEAR POWER?

It produces about 15 percent of the world's electricity. Some people oppose any further increase in nuclear power because its used fuel is very radioactive and hard to dispose of safely.

❯ WHAT IS AN ATOMIC BOMB?

An atomic bomb is one of the two main kinds of nuclear bombs. It relies on the explosive nuclear fission of uranium-235 or plutonium-239. Hydrogen bombs, also called H-bombs, rely on the fusion of hydrogen atoms to create explosions a thousand times more powerful.

❯ WHO INVENTED THE ATOMIC BOMB?

The first atomic bombs were developed in the United States toward the end of World War II by a team of scientists led by Robert Oppenheimer (1904–1967).

TOP ? QUESTION

WHAT IS NUCLEAR FUSION?

Nuclear energy is released by fusing, or joining together, small atoms, such as those of a form of hydrogen called deuterium, often in a reactor (right). Nuclear fusion is the reaction that provides energy for H-bombs. Scientists hope to find a way of harnessing nuclear fusion for power generation.

Water

The properties of water make it extraordinarily useful. In fact, water is essential to life. Without water, plants and animals could not survive. Water can also be harnessed to transport loads and even to generate electricity.

> WHY IS WATER ESSENTIAL FOR LIFE?

Water is chemically neutral, yet dissolves many substances, which is why it is so important for life. Water is found in every cell of the human body. Plants need water for building cells and also for transporting nutrients from the roots to the leaves.

SAILING BOAT

A yacht floats because it is lighter than the water it displaces.

> WHAT'S SO SPECIAL ABOUT WATER?

Water is found naturally as solid ice, liquid water, and gaseous water vapor. This is unusual and happens because of the strong bonds between its two hydrogen and one oxygen atom. When cooled, most substances with similar size atoms to water do not freeze until -22°F. But water freezes at 32°F.

DAM

Hydroelectric power depends on the fact that water is drawn downward by gravity.

➤ WHY DO THINGS FLOAT?

When an object is immersed in water, its weight pushes it down. But the water around it pushes it back up with a force equal to the weight of water displaced (pushed out of the way). So an object will float if it is lighter than, or weighs the same as, the water it displaces.

➤ WHY DO ICEBERGS FLOAT IN THE SEA?

Water is unique in that it expands when it freezes, because the special bonds between its hydrogen atoms begin to break down. This means that ice is lighter (less dense) than water, so icebergs can float.

➤ WHAT IS HYDROELECTRIC POWER?

Hydroelectric power is electricity generated by turbines turned by falling water. Typically, hydroelectric power stations are sited inside dams built to create a big fall in the water.

CAN YOU SQUASH WATER?

Fluids, such as water, cannot be squashed. So if you push a fluid through a pipe, it will push out the other end. Hydraulic power, such as in a forklift truck, uses fluid-filled pipes working like this to lift loads. Hydraulic means "water," but most hydraulic systems use oil to avoid rust problems.

The chemistry of life →

Compounds of carbon atoms form the basis of almost all life processes, from the DNA in our cells to the carbohydrates that we eat for energy. The study of carbon compounds is a vital branch of chemistry.

> WHAT IS ORGANIC CHEMISTRY?

Organic chemistry is the chemistry of carbon and its compounds. Carbon's unique atomic structure means it links atoms together in long chains, rings, or other shapes to form thousands of different compounds. These include complex molecules, such as DNA, that are the basis of life.

DNA CHAIN

The "ropes" of a DNA molecule are made of sugars and phosphates.

> WHAT IS DNA?

DNA is deoxyribonucleic acid. This is the amazing long double-spiral molecule that is found inside every living cell. It is made up of long chains of sugars and phosphates linked by pairs of chemical "bases"—adenine, cytosine, guanine, and thymine. The order in which these bases recur provides in code form the instructions for all the cell's activities, and for the life plan of the entire organism.

> WHO DISCOVERED THE SHAPE OF DNA?

The discovery, in 1953, that every molecule of DNA is shaped like a twisted rope ladder, or "double helix," was one of the great scientific breakthroughs of the twentieth century. Maurice Wilkins and Rosalind Franklin did the groundwork for the discovery. Francis Crick and James Watson, two young researchers at Cambridge University, England, had the inspiration and won the Nobel prize.

> WHAT ARE CARBOHYDRATES?

Carbohydrates are chemicals made only of carbon, hydrogen, and oxygen atoms, including sugars, starches, and cellulose. Most animals rely on carbohydrate sugars, such as glucose and sucrose, for energy.

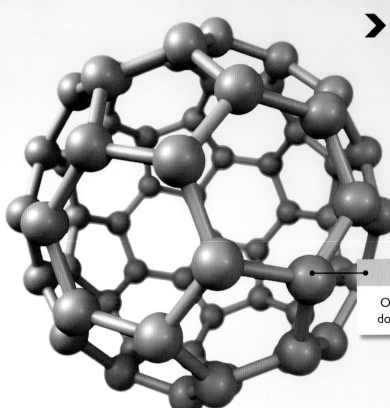

➤ WHAT ARE BUCKYBALLS?

Before 1990, carbon was known in two main forms or allotropes: diamond and graphite. In 1990, a third allotrope was created. Its molecule looks like a soccer ball or the domed stadium roofs created by architect Buckminster Fuller, so this allotrope is called, after him, a buckyball. Buckyballs are so newly discovered that research into their uses is ongoing.

BUCKYBALL

One buckyball contains dozens of carbon atoms.

SYNTHETIC SKIN

Scientists can now manufacture synthetic skin, using polymers, to help people with burns or injuries.

➤ WHAT IS A POLYMER?

Polymers are substances made from long chains of thousands of small carbon-base molecules, called monomers, strung together. Some polymers occur naturally, such as wool and cotton, but plastics, such as nylon and polyethylene, are human-made polymers.

More chemistry of life >

Carbon compounds are important ingredients in a wide range of products that we depend on every day, from plastics and paints to food and medicines. These compounds also contain other elements, such as hydrogen, nitrogen, and oxygen.

CARBON CYCLE
Cows form part of the carbon cycle by eating grass.

> WHAT ARE OILS?

Oils are thick liquids that won't mix with water. Mineral oils used for automobile fuel are hydrocarbons—that is, complex organic chemicals made from hydrogen and carbon.

> WHAT IS THE CARBON CYCLE?

Carbon circulates like this: Animals breathe out carbon as carbon dioxide. Plants take in carbon dioxide from the air and convert it into carbohydrates. When animals eat plants, they take in carbon again.

> HOW IS NATURAL OIL MADE?

Oil is formed from tiny plants and animals that lived in warm seas millions of years ago. As they died, they were slowly buried beneath the seabed. As the seabed sediments hardened into rock, the remains of the organisms were turned to oil and squeezed into cavities in the rock.

OIL PLATFORM
Oil is drilled from the seabed by the workers and machinery on an oil platform.

➤ WHAT IS CELLULOSE?

Cellulose is a natural fiber found in the walls of all plant cells. It is a polymer, made of long chains of sugar molecules. These long chains make it tough and stringy, which is why we can't digest it when we eat plants. It passes through our bodies largely intact.

PLANT CELLS

This image shows the enlarged cellulose-walled cells of a buttercup root.

➤ HOW IS PLASTIC MADE?

Most plastics are made from ethene, one of the products of oil that has been heated under pressure, or cracked. During the process, the ethene molecules join in chains 30,000 or more long. These molecules get tangled like spaghetti. If the strands are held tightly together, the plastic is stiff. If the strands can slip easily over each other, the plastic is flexible, like polyethylene.

➤ WHAT IS A CARBON CHAIN?

Carbon atoms often link together like the links of a chain to form very long, thin molecules, as in the molecule of propane, which consists of three carbon atoms in a row, with hydrogen atoms attached. Propane is commonly used as a fuel for engines and barbecues.

Forces and energy

Forces, energy, and power >

A force is what makes an object move. An important force is gravity, which causes objects to fall to the earth. Energy is the ability to do work. For example, chemical energy fuels a space rocket and allows it to overcome the force of gravity and fly into space.

BLASTOFF
A space rocket overcomes the force of gravity.

> WHAT IS A FORCE?

A force makes something move by pushing or pulling it. Gravity is an invisible force. Other forces, such as a tug-of-war, we can see. Forces work in pairs. For every force pushing in one direction, there is an equal and opposite force pushing in the opposite direction.

> WHAT IS ENERGY?

Energy takes many forms. Heat energy boils water, keeps us warm, and drives engines. Chemical energy fuels cars. Electrical energy drives machines and keeps lights glowing. Light itself is a form of energy (see pp. 98–101). Almost every form of energy can be converted into other forms. But whatever form it is in, energy is essentially the capacity for making something happen, or "doing work."

> WHAT IS POWER?

Power is the rate at which work is done. A high-powered engine is an engine that can move a great deal of weight very quickly. Power is also the rate at which energy is transferred. A large amount of electric power might be needed to heat a large quantity of water.

BRAKE PADS

Brake pads convert a bicycle's movement into heat energy.

TOP QUESTION

WHAT IS FRICTION?

Friction is the force between two things rubbing together, which may be brake pads on a bicycle wheel (above) or air molecules against an airplane. Friction slows things down, making them hot as their momentum, or movement, is converted into heat.

> WHAT IS ENERGY EFFICIENCY?

Some machines waste a great deal of energy, while others waste very little. The energy efficiency of a machine is measured by the proportion of energy it wastes. Waste energy is usually lost as heat.

> WHERE DOES ENERGY COME FROM?

Nearly all our energy comes from the sun. We get some directly by using solar power cells to trap the sun's heat. Most comes indirectly via fossil fuels (coal and oil), which got their energy from the fossilized plants of which they are made. The plants got their energy from the Sun by a process called photosynthesis.

ANTHRACITE COAL

About 40 percent of the world's electricity comes from burning coal. Coal's energy is from the sun.

On the move >

A force, such as a kick or a pull, will set an object in motion. Once an object is moving, it is said to have momentum. Momentum means that an object will always continue moving, unless another force makes it stop.

KICKING A BALL

A ball is given momentum by the force of a kick. It falls to the ground because of the force of gravity.

AROUND AND AROUND

The wind exerts force on the turbine's blades, which exert force on the rest of the windmill, so that it turns on its axis.

> HOW DO THINGS GET MOVING?

Things only move if forced to move. So when something starts moving, there must be a force involved, whether it is visible, such as someone pushing, or gravity, which makes things fall. But once they are moving, things will continue moving at the same speed and in the same direction until another force is applied, typically friction.

> WHAT IS UNIFORM MOTION?

Uniform motion is when an object continues traveling at the same speed in the same direction. This is how a space probe travels when it is not being acted on by gravity or other forces.

➤ WHAT IS A TURNING FORCE?

When something held in one place, called a fulcrum, is pushed or pulled elsewhere, it turns around the fulcrum. When you push a door shut, that push is the turning force, and the hinge is the fulcrum.

➤ WHAT'S THE DIFFERENCE BETWEEN VELOCITY AND SPEED?

Speed is how fast something is going. Velocity is how fast something is going and in which direction. Speed is called a scalar quantity; velocity a vector.

➤ WHY DO THINGS GO AROUND?

If only one force is involved, things will always move in a straight line. This is called linear motion. Things go around when there is more than one force involved. A wheel goes around on its axle because there is one force trying to make it continue in a straight line and another keeping it the same distance from the axle.

LAW OF CONSERVATION OF MOMENTUM

When two objects collide, their combined momentum remains the same if nothing else interferes. So if one object loses momentum, this momentum must be passed on to the other object, making it move. This is called the Law of Conservation of Momentum and can be seen in action with a toy called a Newton's cradle (below).

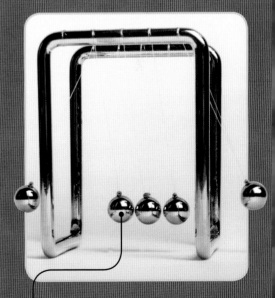

NEWTON'S CRADLE
The balls can be swung so that they knock into each other and pass on their momentum.

Keep moving >

Motion is measured according to its velocity, acceleration, distance traveled, and time taken. Some of the world's greatest scientific minds, including Isaac Newton in the seventeenth century and Albert Einstein in the twentieth century, have considered key questions about motion.

> WHO WAS EINSTEIN?

Albert Einstein (1879–1955; right) was the genius who transformed science with his two big theories: Special Relativity (1905) and General Relativity (1915).

> WHAT IS SPECIAL RELATIVITY?

The theory of Special Relativity shows how space and time can be measured only relatively, that is, in comparison to something else. This means that time can speed up or slow down, depending on how fast you are moving!

ISAAC NEWTON

Newton's studies of motion revolutionized science.

TOP ? QUESTION

WHAT WAS NEWTON'S BREAKTHROUGH?

Sir Isaac Newton's breakthrough in 1687 was to realize that all movement in the universe is governed by three simple rules, which we now call Newton's Laws of Motion (see the opposite page).

CRASH TEST
When a car brakes, momentum carries its passengers forward.

➤ WHAT IS THE DIFFERENCE BETWEEN INERTIA AND MOMENTUM?

Inertia is the tendency of things to stay still unless they are forced to move. Momentum is the tendency for things to keep going once they are moving, unless forced to stop or slow. This is the First Law of Motion.

➤ WHAT HAPPENS WITH EVERY ACTION?

This is Newton's Third Law of Motion: For every action, there is an equal and opposite reaction. This means that whenever something moves, there is a balance of forces pushing in opposite directions. When you push your legs against water to swim, for instance, the water pushes back on your legs equally hard.

➤ WHAT IS ACCELERATION?

Acceleration is how fast something gains speed. The larger the force and the lighter the object, the greater the acceleration. This is Newton's Second Law of Motion.

ACCELERATION
A racing car can accelerate at around 40 miles a second.

Gravity >

Gravity is an invisible force. It is the force of attraction between every part of matter in the universe, such as between the Earth and the sun. Gravity's strength depends on the mass of the objects involved and their distance apart.

HOW DOES GRAVITY HOLD YOU DOWN?

The mutual gravitational attraction between the mass of your body and the mass of the Earth pulls them together. If you jump off a wall, the Earth pulls you toward the ground. You also pull the Earth toward you, but because you are tiny and the Earth is huge, you move a lot and the Earth barely moves at all.

TOP QUESTION

HOW FAST DOES A ROCK FALL?

At first, a rock falls faster and faster at a rate of 32.2 feet per second at every second. But as the rock's speed accelerates, air resistance increases until it becomes so great that the rock cannot fall any faster. It then continues to fall at the same velocity, called the terminal velocity.

WHAT'S THE DIFFERENCE BETWEEN MASS AND WEIGHT?

Mass is the amount of matter in an object. It is the same wherever you measure it, even on the moon. Weight is a measure of the force of gravity on an object. It varies according to where you measure it.

WHY DO SATELLITES GO AROUND THE EARTH?

Satellites are whizzing through space at exactly the right height for their speed. The Earth's gravity tries to pull them down to the Earth, but they are traveling so fast that they go on zooming around the Earth just as fast as the Earth pulls them in.

SATELLITE

A satellite is in uniform motion around the Earth.

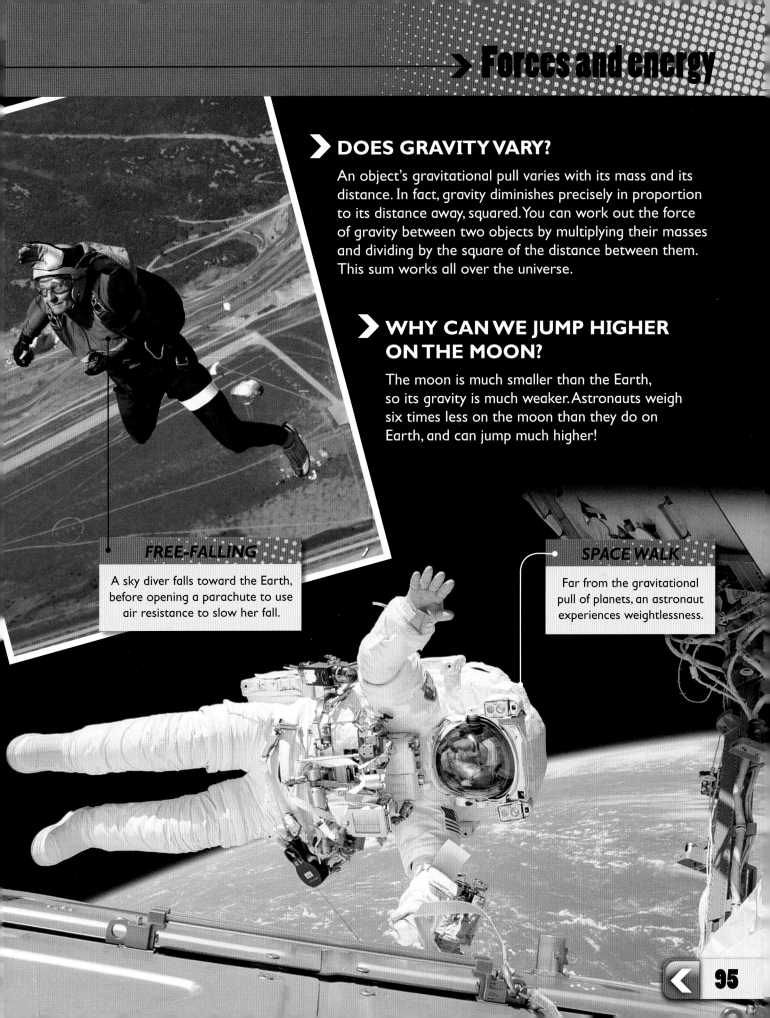

DOES GRAVITY VARY?

An object's gravitational pull varies with its mass and its distance. In fact, gravity diminishes precisely in proportion to its distance away, squared. You can work out the force of gravity between two objects by multiplying their masses and dividing by the square of the distance between them. This sum works all over the universe.

WHY CAN WE JUMP HIGHER ON THE MOON?

The moon is much smaller than the Earth, so its gravity is much weaker. Astronauts weigh six times less on the moon than they do on Earth, and can jump much higher!

FREE-FALLING

A sky diver falls toward the Earth, before opening a parachute to use air resistance to slow her fall.

SPACE WALK

Far from the gravitational pull of planets, an astronaut experiences weightlessness.

Heat >

Heat is a form of energy. It is caused by the movement of molecules. Heat is created by chemical reactions, such as fire; nuclear reactions, such as in the sun; and when other forms of energy, such as electrical or mechanical, are converted into heat, as in friction.

> HOW IS TEMPERATURE MEASURED?

Temperature is usually measured with a thermometer. Some thermometers have a metal strip that bends according to how hot it is. But most contain a liquid, such as mercury, in a tube. As it gets warmer, the liquid expands, and its level rises in the tube. The level of the liquid indicates the temperature.

> WHAT IS THE DIFFERENCE BETWEEN HEAT AND TEMPERATURE?

Heat is molecules moving. It is a form of energy, the combined energy of all the moving molecules. Temperature, on the other hand, is simply a measure of how fast all the molecules are moving.

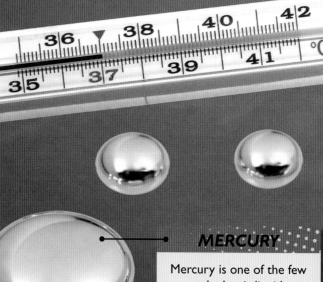

THERMOMETER

As it gets warmer, the molecules of the mercury in the tube move faster, and the mercury expands.

MERCURY

Mercury is one of the few metals that is liquid at room temperature.

❯ WHAT IS ABSOLUTE ZERO?

Absolute zero is the coldest possible temperature, the temperature at which atoms stop moving completely. This happens at -459.67°F, or 0 on the Kelvin scale.

WHAT IS CONDUCTION?

Conduction is one of the three ways in which heat moves. It involves heat spreading from hot areas to cold areas as moving particles knock into one another. The other ways are convection, in which warm air or water rises, and radiation, which is rays of light.

RADIATION

The Sun generates heat by nuclear fusion and radiates it in waves, which we see and feel as sunlight.

CONDUCTION

A hot baking sheet conducts heat and can only be touched safely with mitts.

❯ WHAT IS THE HIGHEST TEMPERATURE EVER RECORDED?

The highest temperature ever measured is 3.6 billion°F. It happened in a nuclear fusion experiment in the United States. The highest air temperature ever recorded is 136°F in Libya. The earth's lowest air temperature ever measured was -128°F. It was recorded in Antarctica. And the lowest temperature ever measured was half a billionth of a degree above absolute zero.

❯ HOW DO YOU CONVERT FAHRENHEIT TO CELSIUS?

You can convert from Fahrenheit to Celsius by subtracting 32, then dividing by nine and multiplying by five. You can convert from Celsius to Fahrenheit by dividing by five, multiplying by nine, and adding 32.

What is light? >

There are many sources of light, including the Sun, lightbulbs, and flames. Light is a form of energy that can be emitted, or radiated, by atoms. Visible light contains all the colors of the rainbow.

> WHAT IS WAVELENGTH?

Light travels in a wavelike manner. Wavelength is the distance between the top of one wave and the next. The different colors of light have different wavelengths. This is shown by a prism, which refracts (bends) light. The longer the wavelength of light, the more it is refracted, so long wavelength colors emerge from the prism at a different point from short wavelength colors.

PRISM

A prism splits light into its different wavelengths.

SPECTRUM

The longest waves of light that we can see are red. The shortest waves of visible light are violet.

WHAT'S THE FASTEST THING IN THE UNIVERSE?

Light, which travels at 186,000 miles per second. This is the one speed in the universe that is constant—that is, it is always the same no matter how fast you are going when you measure it.

WHAT ARE PHOTONS?

Photons are almost infinitesimally small particles of light. They have no mass and there are billions of them in a single beam of light.

RAINBOW

Rainbows occur when the Sun shines through rain.

TOP QUESTION

WHEN IS THE SUN RED?

The Sun is only red at sunrise and sunset, when the Sun is low in the sky and sunlight reaches us only after passing a long way through the dense lower layers of the atmosphere. Particles in the air absorb shorter, bluer wavelengths of light or reflect them away from us, leaving just the red.

WHAT ARE THE COLORS OF THE RAINBOW?

The colors of the rainbow are all the colors contained in white light. When white light hits raindrops in the air, it is split up in the same manner as when it passes through a prism. The colors of the rainbow appear in this order: red, orange, yellow, green, blue, indigo, violet.

WHY IS THE SKY BLUE?

The sky appears to be blue because air molecules scatter—reflect in all directions—more blue from sunlight toward our eyes than the other colors of visible light.

How does light work?

When light hits an object, it can be reflected, absorbed, or bent. The study of light, known as optics, has allowed scientists to discover how we see things. It is light's ability to be reflected that allows us to see.

> HOW IS LIGHT BENT?

Light rays are bent when they are refracted. This happens when they strike a transparent material, such as glass or water, at an angle. The different materials slow the light waves down so that they pivot around, like car wheels driving onto sand.

> HOW DO YOUR EYES SEE THINGS?

Light sources, such as the Sun and electric light, shine light rays straight into your eyes. Everything else you see only by reflected light, that is, by light rays that bounce off things. So you can see things only if there is a light source throwing light onto them. Otherwise, they just look black.

REFRACTION

Water refracts the light, making a straw appear split.

COLORS

A red ball absorbs all the colors except red.

> HOW DO OBJECTS ABSORB LIGHT?

When light rays hit a surface, some bounce off, but others are absorbed by atoms in the surface. Each kind of atom absorbs particular wavelengths, or colors, of light. You see a leaf as green because it has soaked up all colors except green, and you see only the reflected green light.

> DOES LIGHT TRAVEL IN WAVES?

In the last century, most scientists believed that light travels in tiny waves rather than bulletlike particles. Now they agree it can be both, and it is probably best to think of light as vibrating packages of energy.

FIBER-OPTIC CABLES

The cables are used widely in telecommunications to carry messages across long distances.

> HOW DO FIBER-OPTIC CABLES WORK?

These cables don't bend light, but reflect it around corners. Inside a cable are lots of bundles of glass fibers. Light rays zigzag along the inside of each fiber, reflecting first off one side, then the other. In this way, light can be transmitted through the cable no matter what route it takes.

HOW DO MIRRORS WORK?

Most mirrors are made of ordinary glass, but the back is silvered—coated with a shiny metal that reflects all the light that hits it perfectly—at exactly the same angle. The image in a mirror is not, in fact, backward. Left is on the left, and right is on the right—which is the opposite to how we look to someone who is facing us.

REAR VIEW

A car mirror allows us to watch the road behind.

Electromagnetic spectrum >

Light is just a small part of the wide range of radiation emitted by atoms—the only part we can see. This range of radiation is called the electromagnetic spectrum and ranges from long waves, such as radio waves, to short rays, such as gamma rays.

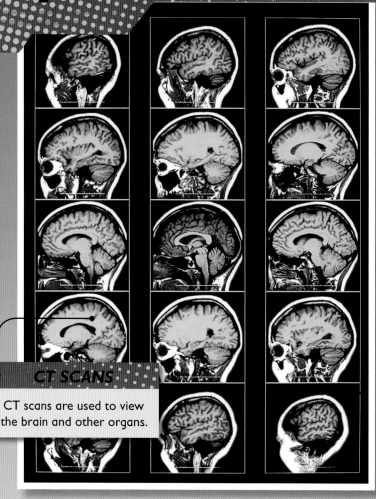

> WHO MADE THE FIRST RADIO BROADCAST?

Italian inventor Guglielmo Marconi first sent radio signals over 5,000 feet in 1895. In 1898, he sent a message in Morse code across the English Channel. (Morse code uses rhythms of short and long sounds to represent letters and numerals.) In 1901, he sent a radio message across the Atlantic Ocean.

CT SCANS
CT scans are used to view the brain and other organs.

> HOW DO CT SCANS WORK?

CT (computed tomography) scans run X-ray beams right around the body, and pick up how much is absorbed with special sensors. A computer analyzes the data to create a complete "slice" through the body.

VISIBLE LIGHT
Visible light has wavelengths of 400 to 700 nanometers (billionths of a meter).

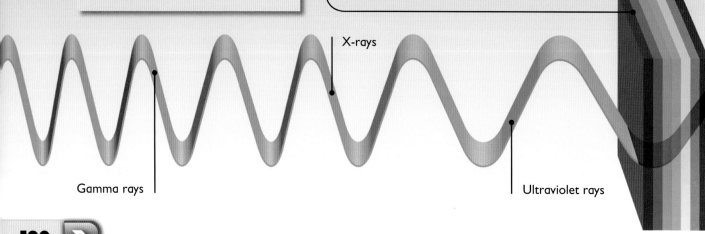

Gamma rays

X-rays

Ultraviolet rays

TOP ? QUESTION

HOW DO TV SIGNALS TRAVEL?

TV signals travel in one of three ways. Terrestrial broadcasts are beamed out from transmitters (right) as radio waves to be picked up by TV antennas. Satellite broadcasts are sent up to satellites as microwaves, then picked up by satellite dishes. Cable broadcasts travel as electrical or light signals along underground cables, straight to the TV set.

TRANSMITTER

Television and radio signals are broadcast by tall transmitters.

> HOW DO X-RAYS PASS THROUGH YOU?

X-rays are stopped only by the bones and especially dense parts of the body. They pass through the soft parts to hit a photographic plate on the far side of the body, where they leave a silhouette of the skeleton.

> WHAT IS INFRARED?

Infrared is light with wavelengths too long for the human eye to register. But you can often feel infrared light as warmth.

> WHY CAN'T YOU SEE ULTRAVIOLET?

Ultraviolet light is light with wavelengths too short for the human eye to register.

Infrared rays

Microwaves

WAVELENGTHS

Wavelengths range from thousands of feet to smaller than an atom.

Radio waves

Electricity >

Electricity is the presence of electrical charge. This charge is carried by electrons and protons in atoms. Electrons have a negative charge and protons a positive one. Electricity can be created naturally, as in lightning, or can be man-made, as with a battery.

> WHAT MAKES LIGHTNING FLASH?

Lightning flashes produce 100 million volts of static electricity. Lightning is created when raindrops and ice crystals inside a thundercloud become electrically charged as they are flung together, losing or gaining electrons from each other. Negatively charged particles build up at the cloud's base, then discharge as lightning.

> WHAT IS AN ELECTRIC CURRENT?

A current is a continuous stream of electrical charge. It happens only when there is a complete, unbroken "circuit" for the current to flow through, typically a loop of copper wire.

LIGHTNING
Lightning flashes to the positively charged ground to discharge its negative electrical charge.

LIGHT SWITCH
Turning on a light switch completes the circuit and allows current to flow to a bulb.

> HOW DO ELECTRIC CURRENTS FLOW?

The charge in an electric current is electrons that have broken free from their atoms. None of them moves very far, but the current is passed on as they bang into each other like rows of marbles.

CHARGE

An electrical charge builds at the base of a thundercloud.

➤ WHAT IS A VOLT?

Electrical current flows as long as there is a difference in charge between two points in the circuit. This difference is called a potential and is measured in terms of volts. The bigger the difference, the bigger the voltage.

➤ WHAT IS RESISTANCE?

Not all substances conduct electric currents equally well. Resistance is a substance's ability to block a flow of electric current. Insulators, such as the plastic around electrical wires, are used for this reason.

TOP QUESTION?

WHAT MAKES YOUR HAIR STAND ON END?

When you comb dry hair, electrons are knocked off the atoms in the comb. Your hair is coated with these negative electrical charges and is attracted to anything positively charged. The same effect occurs if you rub against plastic (right).

Using electricity >

In the late nineteenth century, scientists discovered how to harness electricity to use it as a source of energy. Today, electricity is used to power lighting, industry, transportation, heating, communications, and computers. In the past century, the world has come to rely on electricity to a greater and greater extent.

> WHAT IS A SEMICONDUCTOR?

Semiconductors are materials, such as silicon or germanium, that are partly resistant to electric current and partly conducting. They can be set up so that the conductivity is switched on or off, creating a tiny electrical switch. They are used to make silicon chips, and so are essential to electronics.

> WHAT ARE THE BEST CONDUCTORS?

The best conductors are metals, such as copper and silver. Water is also a good conductor. Superconductors are materials, such as aluminum, which is cooled until it transmits electricity almost without resistance.

COPPER WIRE
Copper is a good conductor. Copper wiring is commonly used to carry electricity through the home.

LIGHTBULB

Thomas Edison invented the first practical bulb in 1879.

WHAT IS A SILICON CHIP?

A silicon chip (below) is an electronic circuit implanted in a small crystal of semiconducting silicon in such a way that it can be manufactured in huge numbers. This was the predecessor to the microprocessors that make computers work.

› HOW DOES A LIGHTBULB WORK?

An electric bulb has a very thin filament of tungsten wire inside a glass bulb filled with argon or nitrogen gas. When current flows through such a thin wire, the resistance is so great that the wire heats up and glows brightly.

› HOW DOES A GENERATOR WORK?

An electricity generator uses mechanical energy to create electrical energy. Many generators use electromagnetic induction, in which a coil of conducting wire, such as copper wire, is spun around inside a magnet. This causes electrons in the wire to move, creating a current.

› WHAT IS "AC"?

"AC" means "alternating current." Electricity in the home is alternating current, which means it continually changes direction as the generator's coil spins around past its electrodes.

Magnetism >

Magnetism is a force that both draws together and pushes apart materials. Certain metals can be strongly magnetic. The electrons in every atom act like tiny magnets, attracting and repelling other electrons. Magnetism occurs when the electrons in an object are all aligned in the same direction.

MAGNET

Metal magnets can occur naturally or be created by stroking them with an existing magnet.

METAL CLIPS

Metal clips are drawn to a magnet. While they are in its magnetic field, the clips become magnetic, too.

> WHAT IS A MAGNETIC POLE?

Some metals, such as iron and nickel, can exert particularly powerful magnetism. This force is especially strong at each end of the magnet. These two powerful ends are called poles.

> WHAT IS A LODESTONE?

Thousands of years before people learned how to make steel magnets, they found that lumps of certain types of rock can attract or repel each other, or parts of iron. These rocks are called lodestones. They contain iron oxide, which makes them naturally magnetic.

➤ WHY IS THE EARTH LIKE A MAGNET?

As the Earth spins, the swirling of its iron core turns the core into a giant magnet. It is a little like the way a bicycle dynamo generates an electric current. Like smaller magnets, the Earth's magnet has two poles, a north and a south. It is because the Earth is a magnet that small magnets always point in the same direction if allowed to swivel freely.

➤ HOW BIG IS THE EARTH'S MAGNETIC FIELD?

The Earth's magnetic field is called the magnetosphere and extends about 43,000 miles toward the Sun.

COMPASS

A magnetized needle always points to the North Pole.

TOP ? QUESTION

WHAT IS A MAGNETIC FIELD?

The magnetic field is the area around the magnet in which its effects are felt. It gets gradually weaker farther away from the magnet. The strength of a magnetic field is measured in teslas, named after the scientist Nikola Tesla.

➤ WHICH MATERIALS MAKE THE STRONGEST MAGNETS?

Due to the arrangement of their electrons, some metals such as iron, nickel, and cobalt, make strong magnets. These metals are also highly attracted to magnets.

MAGNETIC FIELD

A field can be seen when paper is scattered with iron filings.

Sound >

Every sound is created by vibration, whether it is a rubber band twanging or a loudspeaker cone shaking back and forth. Sound reaches your ears as a vibration that travels through the air in waves.

VIOLIN BOW

Drawing a bow across a violin's strings makes them vibrate, creating sound waves.

> HOW DOES SOUND TRAVEL?

When a sound source vibrates back and forth, it pushes the air around it back and forth. The sound then travels through the air as it is pushed back and forth. This moving stretch and squeeze of air is called a sound wave.

> WHAT IS RESONANCE?

An object always tends to vibrate freely at the same rate. This is its natural frequency. You can make it vibrate faster or slower by jiggling it at particular intervals. But if you can jiggle it at just the same rate as its natural frequency, it vibrates in sympathy and the vibrations become stronger. This is resonance.

RESONANCE

The sound made by a violin depends on the resonance of its strings.

❯ WHAT IS SOUND FREQUENCY?

Some sounds, such as a whistle, are high-pitched. Others, such as a drum, are low-pitched. What makes them different is the frequency of the sound waves. If the sound waves follow rapidly after each other, they are high-frequency and make a high sound. If the waves are far apart, they are low-frequency and make a low sound.

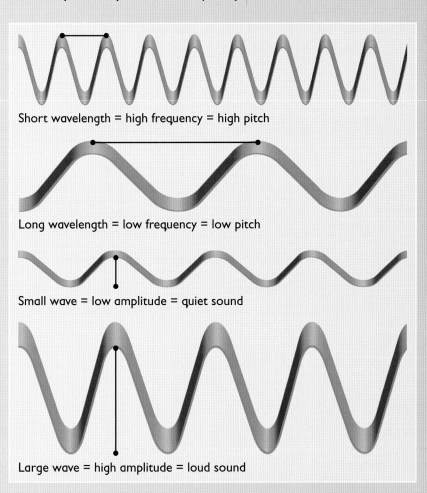

Short wavelength = high frequency = high pitch

Long wavelength = low frequency = low pitch

Small wave = low amplitude = quiet sound

Large wave = high amplitude = loud sound

HOW DO BATS LOCATE THEIR PREY?

Most bats—and some other animals, including whales—locate their prey using echolocation. The bats send out calls, then use the echoes to locate and identify objects. Echolocation is also used for navigating in complete darkness.

BAT CALLS

A bat's echolocation calls are very high frequency.

❯ WHAT IS VOLUME?

The volume of a sound is also called its amplitude. This is the amount of pressure exerted by a sound source on air molecules. The higher the pressure, the harder the molecules will collide and the farther they will travel.

❯ WHAT IS AN ECHO?

An echo is when you shout in a tunnel and you hear the noise bouncing back at you a moment later as the sound waves rebound. Echoes only bounce back clearly off smooth, hard surfaces in confined spaces.

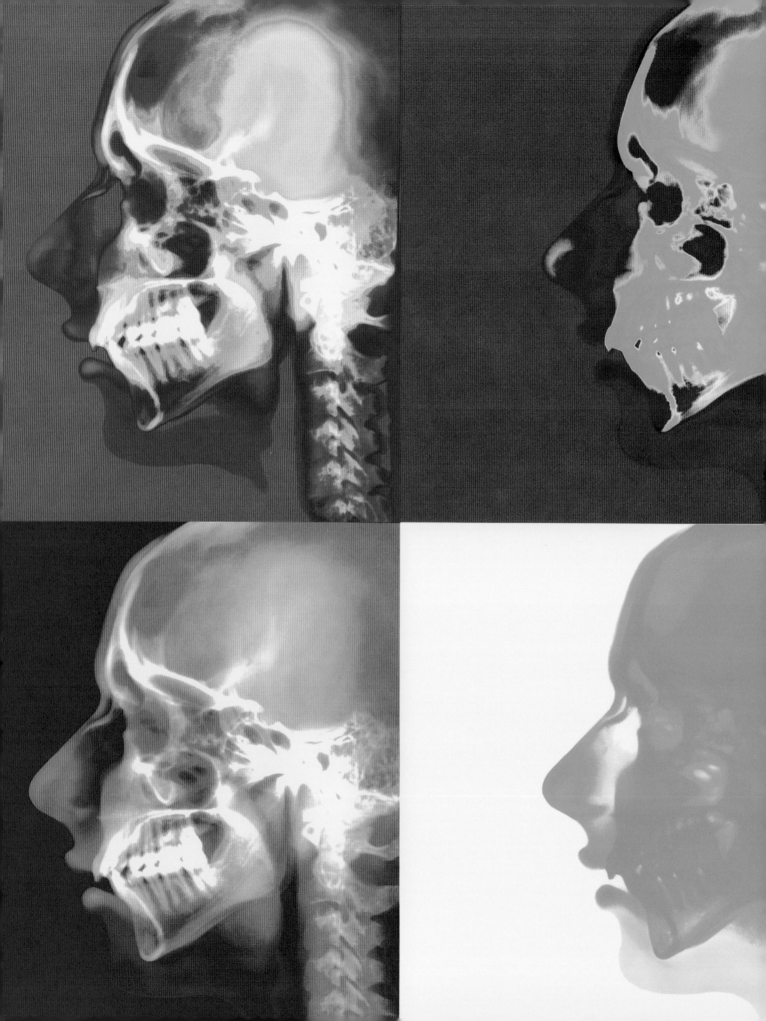

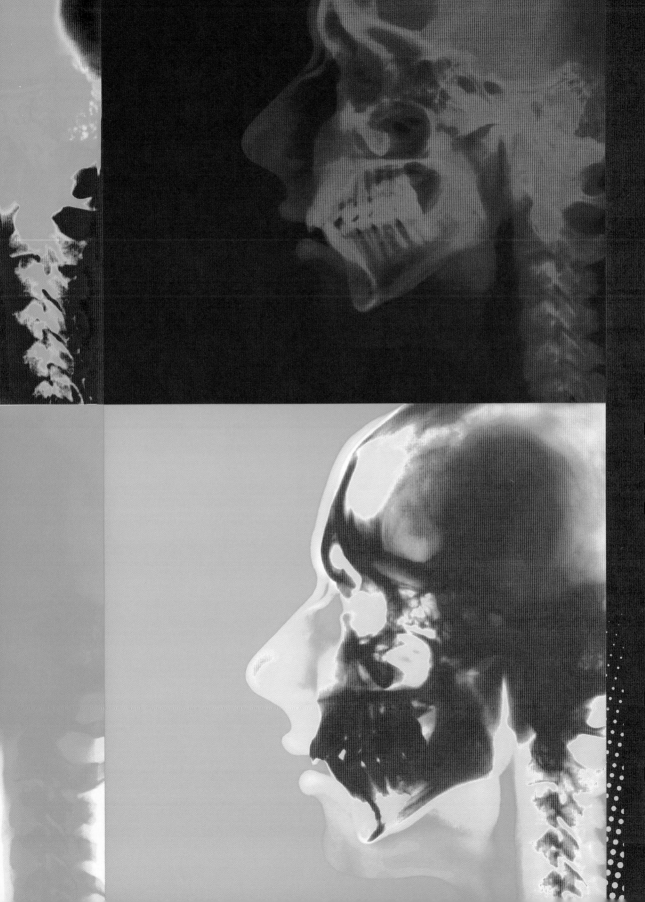

Skin, hair, and nails >

Skin, hair, and nails are part of the body's defenses. Skin forms a protective barrier. Hair keeps us warm. Nails protect our fingers and toes, as well as help us to grasp objects. Skin, hair, and nails contain keratin, a protein that makes them strong.

> WHAT DOES SKIN DO?

Skin stops the moisture inside the body from drying out and prevents germs from getting in. Tiny particles of melanin help to shield your body from the harmful rays of the sun. The more melanin you have, the darker your skin, and the better protected you are.

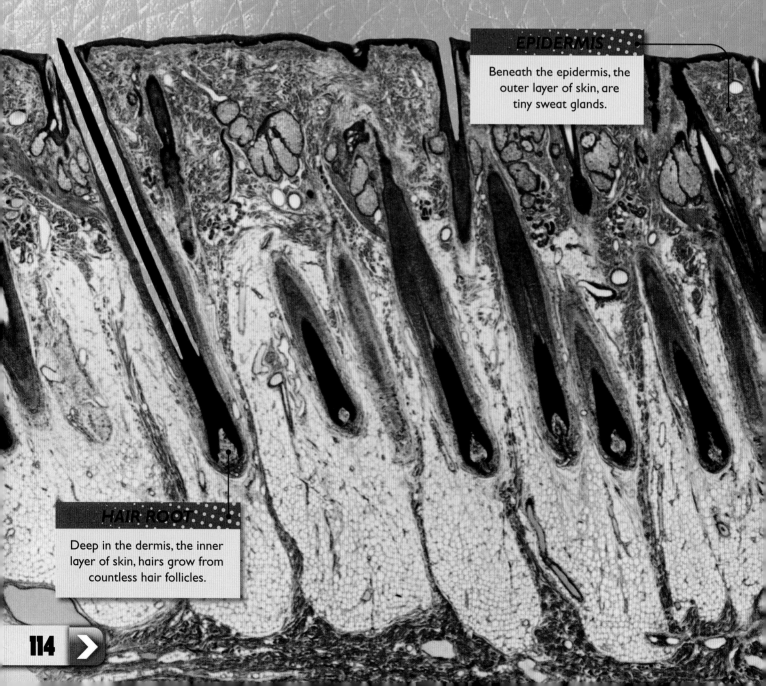

EPIDERMIS

Beneath the epidermis, the outer layer of skin, are tiny sweat glands.

HAIR ROOT

Deep in the dermis, the inner layer of skin, hairs grow from countless hair follicles.

> WHY DOES HAIR FALL OUT?

No hair lasts more than about six years. Every day you lose about 60 hairs, but since you have about 100,000 on your scalp, you hardly notice. After a while, new hairs grow from hair follicles.

> WHAT GIVES HAIR ITS COLOR?

The color of your hair is determined mainly by the pigment (colored substance) it contains. Hair color depends on melanin, which is a pigment in two forms: one lighter, causing blond or red hair, the other darker, causing brown or black hair.

MAGNIFIED HAIR

The hair shaft is protected by a hard outer layer.

> WHY DOES SKIN HAVE PORES?

Skin has tiny holes, called sweat pores, to let out sweat. When you are too hot, glands pump out sweat, or water, which cools you as it evaporates.

> HOW FAST DO NAILS GROW?

A fingernail grows about one twenty-fifth of an inch every 7 days. As new nail forms behind the cuticle, under the skin, it pushes the older nail along.

FINGERPRINT

The uniqueness of fingerprints has led to their being used for identification.

TOP QUESTION

ARE FINGERPRINTS UNIQUE?

Yes! A fingerprint is made by thin ridges of skin on the tip of each finger and thumb. The ridges form a pattern of lines, loops, or whorls, and no two people have the same pattern.

Bones provide a strong framework that supports the body and protects the brain, lungs, and other vital organs. You can move and bend different parts of the body because the bones meet at joints.

> WHAT IS A JOINT?

Where two bones meet, their ends are shaped to make different kinds of joints. Each kind of joint makes a strong connection and allows a particular kind of movement. For example, the knee is a hinge joint that lets the lower leg move only back and forward. The hip is a ball-and-socket joint that allows you to move your thigh in a circle.

THE SKELETON

All the bones together are called the skeleton. An adult has about 206 bones.

> WHY DON'T JOINTS SQUEAK?

Joints are cushioned by soft, squashy cartilage. Many joints also contain synovial fluid, which works like oil to keep them moving smoothly and painlessly.

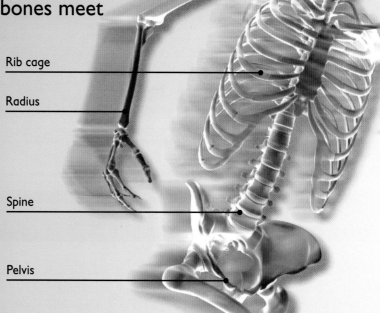

Skull

Rib cage

Radius

Spine

Pelvis

Femur (thighbone)

Patella (kneecap)

Tibia (shin)

Fibula

Metatarsals (toe bones)

BROKEN BONE

Bones can break because of a fall or accident. A break will mend fully in up to 18 months.

HOW MANY VERTEBRAE ARE THERE IN THE SPINE?

A vertebra is a knobbly bone in your spine. The 33 vertebrae fit together to make a strong pillar, the spine, which carries much of your weight.

➤ WHICH IS THE LONGEST BONE?

The femur, or thighbone, in the upper part of the leg is the longest bone in the body. It accounts for more than a quarter of an adult's height.

➤ WHAT IS INSIDE A BONE?

Inside the larger bones is a crisscross honeycomb. Blood vessels weave in and out of the bone, keeping the cells alive.

➤ WHAT ARE LIGAMENTS?

They are strong, flexible straps that hold together the bones in a joint. Nearly all the body's joints have several ligaments.

VERTEBRAE X-RAY

The discovery that X-rays can be used to photograph bones was made over 100 years ago.

Muscles >

The skeleton is covered with muscles that move your bones and give your body its shape. Muscles in the legs allow us to run, jump, and kick. Different kinds of muscles make the heart beat and move food through the intestines.

> HOW DO MUSCLES WORK?

Muscles work by contracting. Each muscle is connected to at least two bones. When they contract, muscles get shorter and thicker and so they pull the bones together, causing the body to move.

> WHICH IS THE BIGGEST MUSCLE?

The biggest muscle is the gluteus maximus in the buttock. You can use it to straighten your leg when you stand up, and it makes a comfortable pillow to sit on.

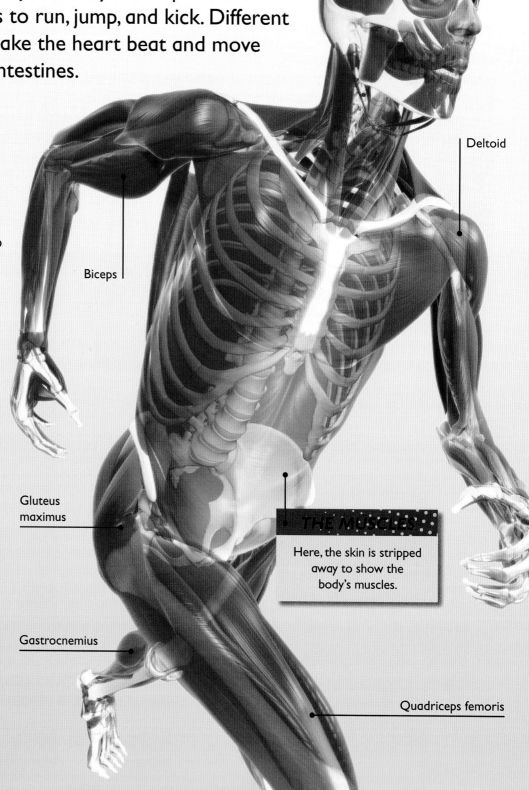

Deltoid

Biceps

Gluteus maximus

Gastrocnemius

Quadriceps femoris

THE MUSCLES

Here, the skin is stripped away to show the body's muscles.

WHY DOES EXERCISE MAKE MUSCLES STRONGER?

A muscle is made of bundles of fibers that contract when you use the muscle. The more you use the muscle, the thicker the fibers become. They contract more effectively, which means the muscle is stronger.

❯ WHY DO MUSCLES WORK IN PAIRS?

Because muscles cannot push, they can only pull. For example, to bend your elbow, you tighten the biceps muscle at the front of your upper arm. To straighten the elbow again, you relax the biceps and tighten the triceps muscle at the back of your upper arm.

❯ WHAT IS A TENDON?

A tendon is like a rope that joins a muscle to a bone. If you bend and straighten your fingers, you can feel the tendons in the back of your hand. The body's strongest tendon is the Achilles tendon, which is above your heel.

❯ HOW MANY MUSCLES ARE THERE IN THE BODY?

You have about 650 muscles that work together. Most actions—including walking, swimming, and smiling—involve dozens of muscles.

STRETCHING

Regular stretching of muscles can make them more flexible.

The nervous system >

Nerves carry information and instructions to and from the brain. Sensory nerves bring information from the eyes, ears, and other sense organs to the brain. The motor nerves control the muscles, telling them when to contract.

SPINAL CORD

The spinal cord is the body's largest nerve. It runs through the center of the spine.

> HOW DOES SMELL WORK?

A smell is made by tiny particles in the air. When you breathe in, these particles dissolve in mucus in the nose. Smell receptors in the nose respond to this and send a message to the brain.

NERVOUS SYSTEM

Hundreds of nerves reach out to all parts of the body. They are connected to the brain by the spinal cord.

> WHAT ARE THE BODY'S FIVE MAIN SENSES?

The five main senses are seeing, hearing, smelling, tasting, and touching. Each sense has a special part of the body, called a sense organ, which reacts to a particular kind of stimulus. For example, eyes react to light and ears react to sound.

> HOW DOES TOUCH WORK?

There are many different kinds of sense receptors in the skin, which between them react to touch, heat, cold, and pain. The brain puts together all the different messages to tell you if something is shiny, wet, cold, and many other things.

> CAN BLIND PEOPLE USE TOUCH TO READ?

Yes. Blind people can run their fingertips over Braille (right)—a pattern of raised dots that represent different letters.

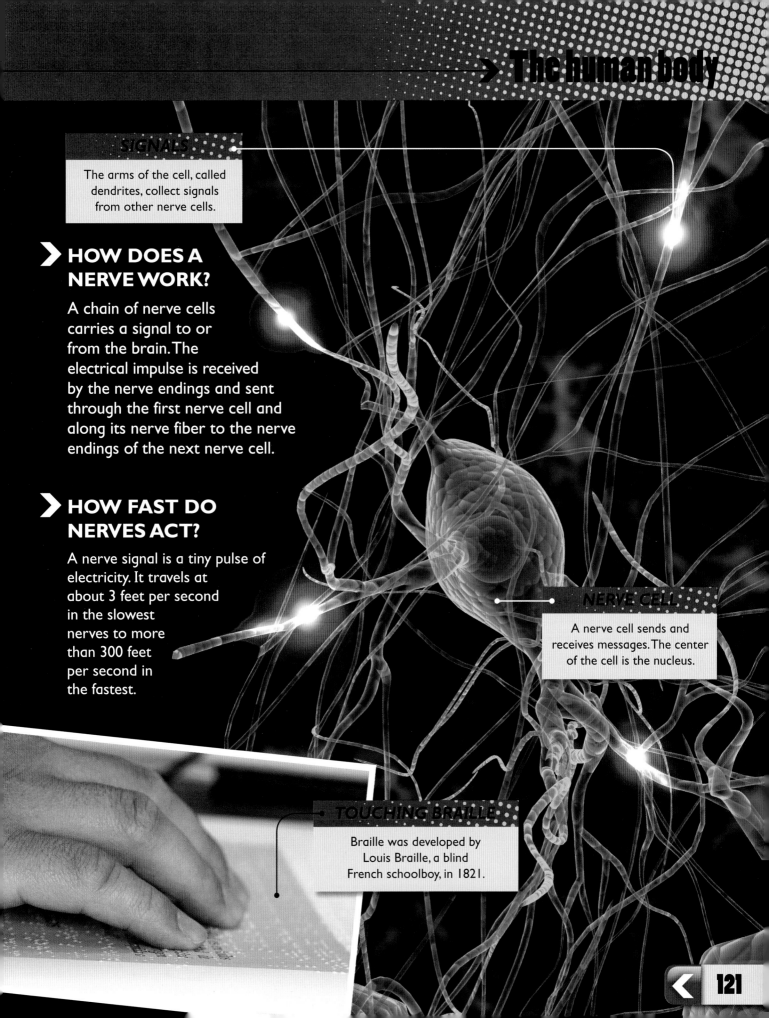

SIGNALS

The arms of the cell, called dendrites, collect signals from other nerve cells.

➤ HOW DOES A NERVE WORK?

A chain of nerve cells carries a signal to or from the brain. The electrical impulse is received by the nerve endings and sent through the first nerve cell and along its nerve fiber to the nerve endings of the next nerve cell.

➤ HOW FAST DO NERVES ACT?

A nerve signal is a tiny pulse of electricity. It travels at about 3 feet per second in the slowest nerves to more than 300 feet per second in the fastest.

NERVE CELL

A nerve cell sends and receives messages. The center of the cell is the nucleus.

TOUCHING BRAILLE

Braille was developed by Louis Braille, a blind French schoolboy, in 1821.

Your brain controls your body, keeping the vital organs working, collecting information from the senses, and sending messages to the muscles. The brain also controls everything you think and feel, as well as storing memories of the past.

❯ WHAT DOES THE CEREBRAL CORTEX DO?

The cortex is the wrinkly top part of the brain. It controls all the brain activity that you are aware of—seeing, thinking, reading, feeling, and moving. Only humans have such a large and well-developed cerebral cortex. Different parts of the cortex deal with different activities. The left side controls the right side of the body, while the right side of the cortex controls the left side of the body.

CORTEX

This part of the cerebral cortex controls vision and recognition of colors.

CEREBELLUM

The cerebellum coordinates movement and maintains balance.

TOP ? QUESTION

WHAT DOES THE SKULL DO?

The skull is a hard covering of bone that protects the brain like a helmet. All the bones of the skull except the lower jaw are fused together to make them stronger.

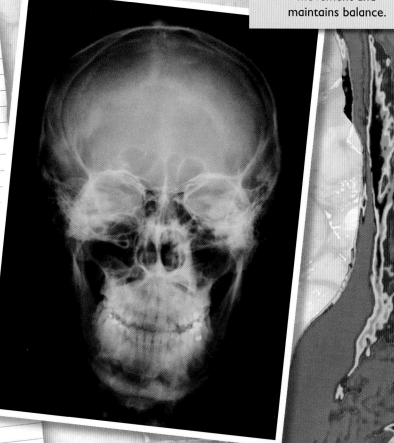

> WHY DO YOU REMEMBER SOME THINGS AND FORGET OTHERS?

You usually remember things that are important to you in some way. Some things need to be remembered for only a short while. For instance, you might look up a telephone number, keep it in your head while you dial, and then forget it.

HYPOTHALAMUS

The hypothalamus controls hunger, thirst, and body temperature.

> WHY ARE SOME PEOPLE LEFT-HANDED?

Most people are right-handed—the left side of their brain is dominant. In left-handed people, the right side of the brain is dominant. The part of the brain that controls speech is usually on the dominant side.

> WHY DO SOME PEOPLE SLEEPWALK?

People may walk in their sleep because they are worried or anxious. If someone is sleepwalking, you should gently take them back to bed.

SLEEPING

The brain blocks most incoming signals while you sleep, unless they are so strong that they wake you up.

> WHY DO YOU NEED TO SLEEP?

The truth is that scientists don't yet really know! Sleeping performs some mental function still to be identified. A ten-year-old sleeps an average of nine or ten hours a night, but sleep time can vary between 4 and 12 hours.

You see an object when light bounces off it and enters your eyes. The black circle in the middle of the eye is called the pupil. Light passes through the pupil and is focused by the lens onto the retina at the back of the eye. The retina sends signals to the brain.

> HOW DO YOU SEE COLOR?

Different nerve cells in the retina, called cones, react to the colors red, blue, and green. Together they make up all the colors. The cones only work well in bright light, which is why you can't see color when it gets dark.

THE EYE

The eye is protected by the eyelid. The eyelashes prevent dust and dirt from entering.

Eyelashes

Sclera (white of the eye)

Iris

> WHY DO YOU BLINK?

You blink to clean your eyes. Each eye is covered with a thin film of salty fluid, so every time you blink, the eyelid washes the eyeball and wipes away dust and germs. The water drains away through a narrow tube into the nose.

Tear duct

Pupil

➤ WHY DO YOU HAVE TWO EYES?

Two eyes help you to judge how far away something is. Each eye gets a slightly different picture, which the brain combines into a single three-dimensional or 3D, picture—one that has depth as well as height and breadth.

➤ WHY DOES THE PUPIL CHANGE SIZE?

The pupil becomes smaller in bright light to stop too much light from damaging the retina. In dim light, the pupil opens to let in more light. The iris is a circular muscle that controls the size of the pupil.

EYEBALL

Nerves in the retina send signals along the optic nerve to the brain.

TOP QUESTION

HOW BIG IS AN EYEBALL?

An adult eyeball is about the size of a golf ball, but most of the eyeball is hidden inside your head.

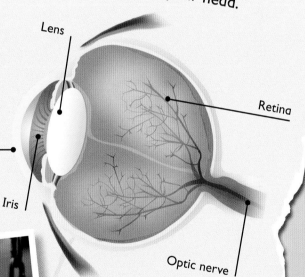

Lens

Retina

Iris

Optic nerve

➤ WHY DO PEOPLE HAVE DIFFERENT COLORED EYES?

The iris is the colored ring around the pupil. The color is made by a substance called melanin. Brown irises have a lot of melanin, while blue irises have a little. Very occasionally, someone has irises of different colors (left).

The ears >

Sound reaches your ears as vibrations in the air. The vibrations travel to the eardrum, which makes the bones in the middle ear vibrate, too. These pass the vibrations to the fluid around the cochlea in the inner ear. Nerve endings in the cochlea send signals to the brain.

> HOW DO EARS HELP YOU TO BALANCE?

Three tubes in the inner ear, called the semicircular canals, are filled with fluid. As you move, the fluid inside them moves. Nerves in the lining of the tubes detect changes in the fluid and send signals to the brain.

TOP QUESTION ?

HOW IS SOUND MEASURED?

The loudness of a sound is measured in decibels. The sound of a pin dropping is less than 10 decibels, while a personal stereo makes about 80 decibels. A noise over 120 decibels can damage your hearing.

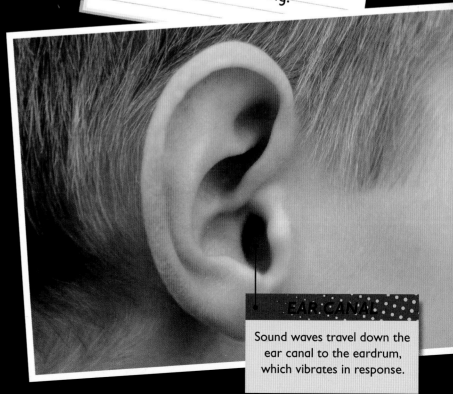

BALANCING

A gymnast balances with the help of semicircular tubes in the inner ear.

EAR CANAL

Sound waves travel down the ear canal to the eardrum, which vibrates in response.

WHY DO YOU GET DIZZY?

If you spin around and around and then stop, the world seems to continue spinning. This is because the fluid in the semicircular canals is still moving as though you were still spinning.

INNER EAR

The cochlea is filled with fluid and lined with nerve endings, which take signals to the brain.

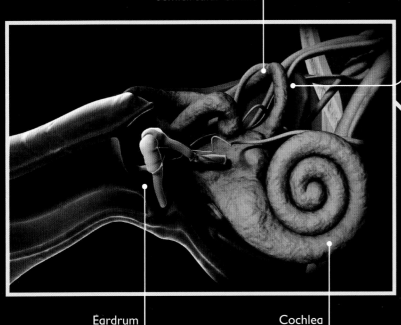

Semicircular canals

Eardrum

Cochlea

OUTER EAR

The outer ear is known as the auricle, or pinna.

WHAT IS EARWAX?

This yellow-brown wax is made by glands in the skin lining the ear canal. Wax traps dirt and germs and is slowly pushed out of the ear.

WHY DO YOU HAVE TWO EARS?

Two ears help you to detect which direction sounds are coming from.

WHY DO YOUR EARS POP?

If you are flying in an aircraft and it changes height quickly, you may go a little deaf, because the air inside and outside the eardrum are at different pressures. Your ears "pop" when the pressures become equal again.

The digestive system >

The digestive system breaks down food into simple nutrients that the body can absorb. The process starts when we chew and swallow food, continues in the stomach and intestines, and ends when waste products are expelled from the body as feces.

> WHAT HAPPENS TO THE FOOD WE EAT?

After it is swallowed, food goes down the esophagus into the stomach. Here it is broken down into a soupy liquid, before being squeezed through a coiled tube called the small intestine. The nourishing parts of the food are absorbed into the blood and the rest passes into the large intestine. About 24 hours after swallowing, the waste, called feces, is pushed out of the body.

> HOW DO YOU DETECT TASTE?

As you chew, tiny particles of food dissolve in saliva and trickle down to the taste buds on the tongue. The taste receptors react and send messages about the taste to the brain.

TASTE BUDS

The tongue has about 10,000 microscopic taste buds. Buds on different parts of the tongue react to different tastes.

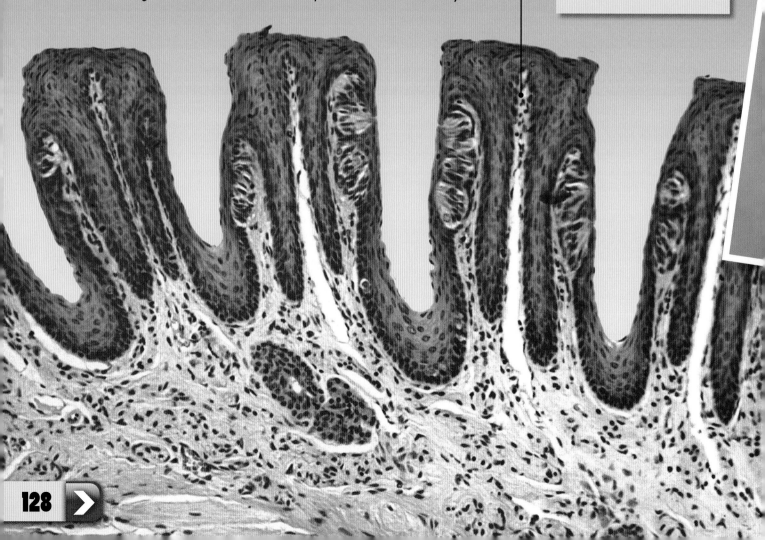

> WHY DOES VOMIT TASTE REALLY SOUR?

When you vomit, you bring partly digested food into your mouth. It is sour because it is mixed with acid made by the stomach lining. The acid helps to break down food into smaller pieces.

> WHAT IS THE EPIGLOTTIS?

The epiglottis is a kind of trap door that closes off your windpipe when you swallow. It stops food from going down into the lungs, rather than down the esophagus to the stomach.

HOW LONG ARE THE INTESTINES?

The small intestine is more than three times as long as the whole body! In an adult, this is about 20 feet. The large intestine is a further 5 feet, and the whole tube from mouth to anus measures around 30 feet.

CHEWING

When you chew food, it becomes a mushy ball, ready to travel down the esophagus.

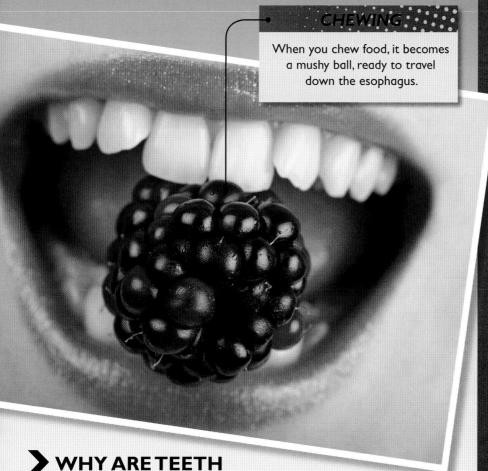

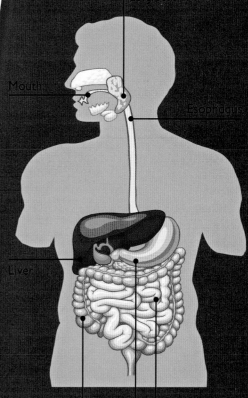

Epiglottis

Mouth

Esophagus

Liver

Large intestine

Stomach

Small intestine

> WHY ARE TEETH DIFFERENT SHAPES?

Different teeth do different jobs to help you to chew up food. The broad, flat teeth at the front slice through food when you take a bite. They are called incisors. The pointed canine teeth grip and tear chewy food, such as meat. The large premolars and molars grind the food between them into small pieces.

The lungs and breathing >

The air contains oxygen, which the body needs to stay alive. When you breathe in, you pull air through the mouth or nose into the windpipe and down to the lungs. Here the oxygen is passed into the blood, then carried to all parts of the body.

> HOW LONG CAN YOU HOLD YOUR BREATH?

You can probably hold your breath for about a minute. The longer you hold your breath, the higher the carbon dioxide level in your blood rises, and the more you feel the need to breathe out.

> WHAT HAPPENS TO AIR IN THE LUNGS?

The air you breathe in travels from the windpipe into bronchioles, or tiny tubes, in the lungs. At the end of each bronchiole are minute balloons called alveoli. As these balloons fill with air, oxygen passes from them into the blood vessels that surround them. The blood then carries the oxygen around the body. At the same time, waste carbon dioxide passes out of the blood and into the lungs. It leaves the body in the air you breathe out.

BREATH CLOUD

The air you breathe out contains water vapor. On a cold day, this condenses into a mist of tiny water droplets.

> WHY DO YOU COUGH?

You cough when mucus, dust, or other particles clog the air passages between your nose and lungs. The sudden blast of air helps to clear the tubes.

➤ HOW DO YOU TALK?

When you breathe out, the air passes over the vocal cords in the larynx, or voice box, in the neck. When the cords vibrate, they make a sound. Changing the shape of your lips and tongue makes different sounds, which can be put together into words.

➤ WHY DOES RUNNING MAKE YOU PUFF?

Muscles use up oxygen as they work. When you run, your muscles are working hard and need extra oxygen. Puffing makes you breathe in up to 20 times more air to supply your muscles with the oxygen they need.

WHY DO THE LUNGS HAVE SO MANY ALVEOLI?

In order to provide a huge surface across which oxygen and carbon dioxide can move in and out of the blood. In fact, the lungs have more than 700 million alveoli.

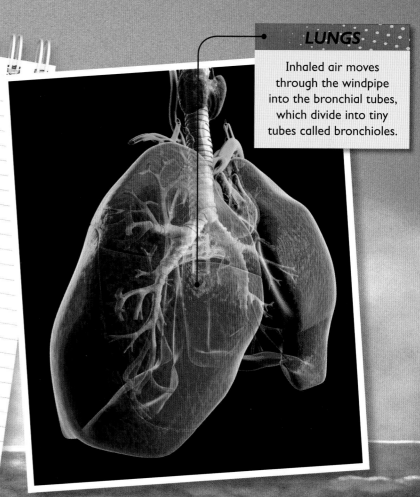

LUNGS

Inhaled air moves through the windpipe into the bronchial tubes, which divide into tiny tubes called bronchioles.

The heart and blood

The heart's job is to pump blood to the lungs and then all around the body. The right side of the heart takes in blood from the body and pumps it to the lungs. The left side takes blood filled with oxygen from the lungs and pumps it around the body.

> HOW OFTEN DOES THE HEART BEAT?

A child's heart usually beats about 80 times a minute, a little faster than an adult's (70 times a minute). When you run or do something strenuous, your heart beats faster to send more blood to the muscles.

RED BLOOD CELL

Each tiny drop of blood contains up to 5 million red blood cells. These are the most common type of blood cell.

> WHY IS BLOOD RED?

Blood gets its color from billions of red blood cells. These cells contain a substance called hemoglobin, which absorbs oxygen in the lungs. Blood that is rich in oxygen is bright red, and as it is pumped around the body, the oxygen is gradually taken up by the body's cells. By the time the blood returns to the heart, it is a darker, more rusty red.

TOP QUESTION ?

WHAT DO WHITE BLOOD CELLS DO?

They surround and destroy germs and other intruders that get into the blood.

DEFENSE

White blood cells are part of the immune system, protecting us from infection.

> WHAT IS PLASMA?

Just over half the blood is a yellowish liquid called plasma. It is mainly water with molecules of digested food and essential salts dissolved in it.

> WHAT IS THE HEART MADE OF?

A special kind of muscle, called cardiac (heart) muscle, which never gets tired.

Artery

Vein

> WHAT IS A CAPILLARY?

Blood travels around the body through tubes called arteries and veins. These branch off into smaller tubes that reach every cell of the body. Capillaries are the tiniest blood vessels of all. Most capillaries are thinner than a single hair.

CARDIOVASCULAR SYSTEM

Oxygen-rich blood leaves the heart along arteries (red in this diagram) and used blood returns along veins (in blue).

The kidneys and liver >

The kidneys filter the blood to remove wastes and extra water and salts. The liver is a chemical factory that does more than 500 different jobs, including the processing of food and the removal of wastes and poisons from the blood.

> WHAT IS URINE?

Each kidney has about a million tiny filters, which between them clean about a quarter of your blood every minute. The unwanted substances combine with water to make urine, which trickles down to the bladder.

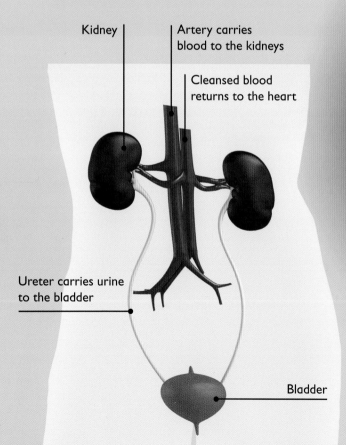

Kidney

Artery carries blood to the kidneys

Cleansed blood returns to the heart

Ureter carries urine to the bladder

Bladder

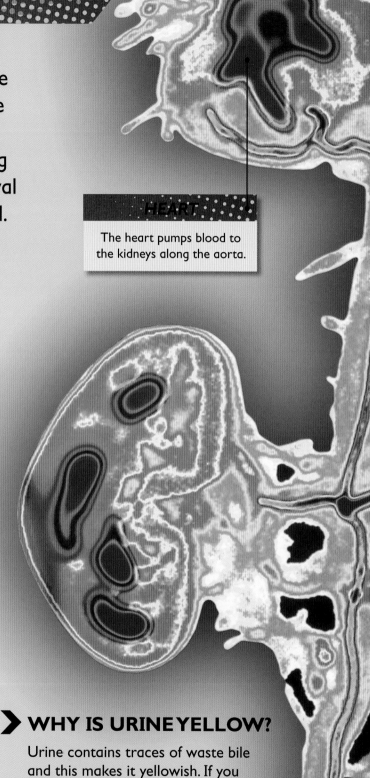

HEART
The heart pumps blood to the kidneys along the aorta.

> WHY IS URINE YELLOW?

Urine contains traces of waste bile and this makes it yellowish. If you drink a lot of water, your urine will be diluted and less yellow. Some foods affect the color of urine. For example, eating beets can turn it pinkish.

WHAT DOES THE LIVER DO?

One of the liver's most important functions is the processing of digested food (see the diagram on p. 129). The intestines pass digested food to the liver, where some nutrients may be released into the blood and the rest stored to be used later. The liver also processes poisons in the blood and changes unwanted proteins into urea. The kidneys then remove poisons and urea from the blood and make them into urine.

WHAT IS BILE?

Bile is a yellow-green liquid made by the liver and stored in the gallbladder. From there it passes into the small intestine, where it helps to break up fatty food.

KIDNEYS

This medical thermographic image shows raised temperatures caused by activity in the body. It reveals the kidneys at work, processing the blood.

WHY DO YOU SWEAT WHEN YOU ARE HOT?

Sweating helps to cool you down. When the body becomes hot, sweat glands pump lots of salty water onto the skin. As the sweat evaporates, it takes extra heat from the body.

SWEATING

When you exercise, the body gets hot, making you sweat. Drinking replaces the lost water.

TOP QUESTION

HOW MUCH DO YOU NEED TO DRINK?

You need to drink about 2½–3 pints (5 large glasses) of watery drinks a day. Most water is lost in urine and feces, but sweat and the air you breathe also contain water.

A baby begins when a sperm from a man joins with an egg from a woman. The cells of the fertilized egg embed in the lining of the mother's womb. Slowly the cells multiply into the embryo of a new human being.

> WHERE DOES A MAN'S SPERM COME FROM?

Sperm are made in the testicles, two sacs that hang on either side of the penis. After puberty, the testicles make millions of sperm every day. Any sperm that are not ejaculated are absorbed back into the blood.

> WHAT IS A FETUS?

A fetus is an unborn baby from eight weeks after conception until birth. In the first seven weeks, it is called an embryo. From about 24 weeks onward, babies may survive in an incubator if they are born early, but most stay in the mother's womb for the full 38 weeks.

PREGNANCY

A baby usually grows in its mother's womb for 38 weeks.

> WHERE DOES THE EGG COME FROM?

When a girl is born she already has thousands of eggs stored in her two ovaries. After puberty, one of these eggs is released every month and travels down the Fallopian tube to the womb.

> HOW DOES AN UNBORN BABY FEED?

Most of the cluster of cells that embeds itself in the womb grows into an organ called the placenta. Food and oxygen from the mother's blood pass through the placenta into the blood of the growing baby.

NEWBORN

The average newborn weighs about 7¾ pounds. Most newborns like to sleep a lot.

HOW FAST DOES AN UNBORN BABY GROW?

You grow faster before you are born than at any other time. Three weeks after the egg is fertilized, the embryo is the size of a grain of rice. Five weeks later, almost every part of the baby has formed—the brain, eyes, heart, stomach—yet it is only the size of a thumb. By the time it is born, the baby will probably be about 20 inches long.

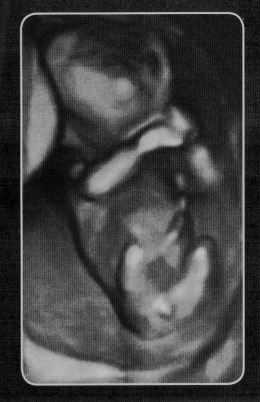

> WHAT ARE GENES?

Genes are a combination of chemicals contained in each cell. They come from your mother and father and determine all your physical characteristics, including the color of your hair, how tall you will be, and even what diseases you might get later in life.

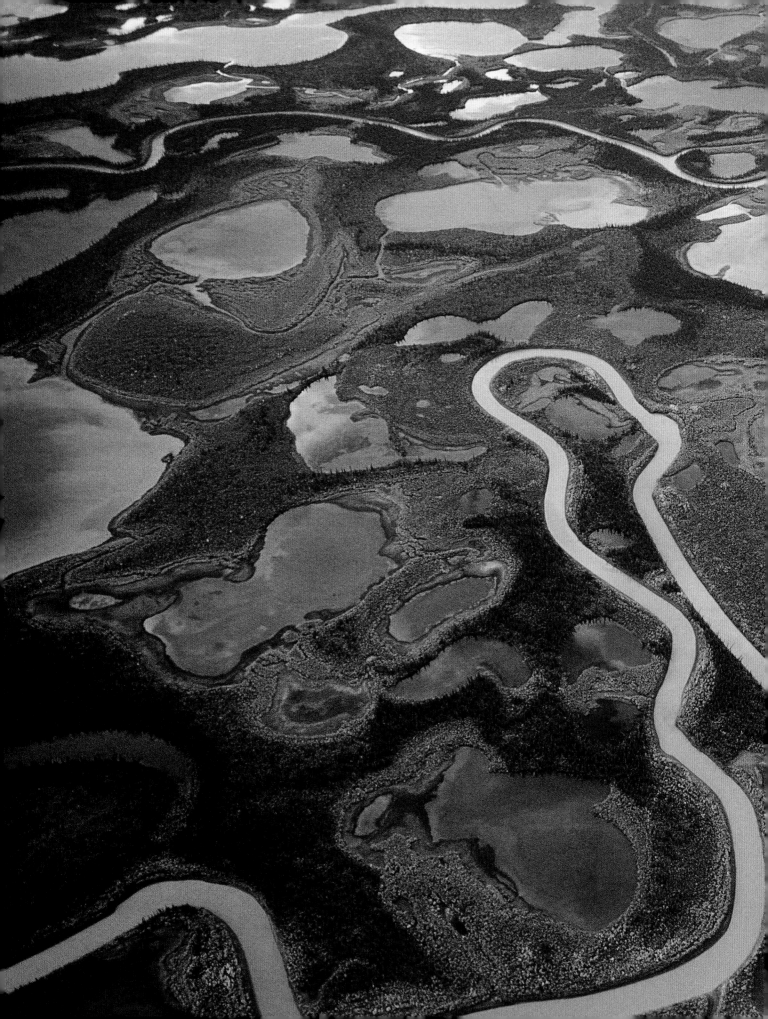

Ecosystems

Desert →

A desert is an area that receives very little rain and so is unable to support much plant growth. Although many deserts are in hot regions, some of the world's deserts can be extremely cold.

❯ WHICH IS THE DRIEST DESERT?

Most areas of the Sahara have around 3 inches of rainfall in an average year, making this one of the driest deserts. Parts of the Atacama Desert in Chile are also very dry. Several years may pass between rainfalls there.

SAHARA
The dry central region of the Sahara is covered by vast sand dunes.

❯ WHICH IS THE HOTTEST DESERT?

Parts of the Sahara, in North Africa, and the Mojave Desert, in the southwestern United States, experience very high temperatures. The average summer temperature may be over 100°F. In Death Valley in the Mojave Desert, temperatures of 135°F have been recorded.

❯ WHICH IS THE BIGGEST DESERT?

The Sahara in North Africa covers an area of about 3,615,000 square miles. This is nearly as big as the United States.

Antarctica is sometimes called a cold desert, and is in fact extremely dry, because all its water is locked up as ice. The deserts of Central Asia—in Mongolia and western China—are chilled in winter by cold air from the Arctic. Even in summer, when the days are hot, the temperature can drop to below freezing at night.

❯ WHAT IS A RAIN SHADOW?

A rain shadow is a dry region of land that lies close to a mountain range. The mountains block the passage of rain-bringing clouds, casting a "shadow" of dryness. The Gobi Desert (above), in Central Asia, is in the shadow of the Himalayan Mountains.

❯ WHY ARE SOME DESERTS EXPANDING?

The Sahara is growing larger each year, partly because the climate is getting gradually warmer, but mainly because the plant life on the edges of the desert has been destroyed by grazing animals.

ANTARCTIC DESERT

The continent is too dry and cold to support much plant life. Only moss, lichen, and algae can grow.

Desert plants

The key problem faced by desert plants is lack of water. Plants must survive months—or even years—of drought. Some desert plants store water in their leaves, roots, and stems.

WHAT IS AN OASIS?

An oasis is a place in the desert where water is in plentiful supply, such as at a pool permanently fed by a spring. Many plants can grow at an oasis, even in the heat of the desert. Date palms are commonly planted at oases, both for shade and to provide fruit.

WHAT LIVES IN A LARGE CACTUS?

Cacti are home to a variety of wildlife. Their flowers are visited by butterflies, moths, and hummingbirds. Holes in cactus stems provide nest sites for desert rodents and for birds, such as the tiny elf owl.

HOW DOES A CACTUS SURVIVE IN THE DESERT?

Cacti have generally leafless, swollen stems that store water. Since they lack leaves, they do not lose much water through evaporation. Most cacti are spiny, which probably protects them from being eaten by hungry and thirsty desert animals.

DESERT OASIS

An oasis is a source of vital water, where trees, bushes, grasses, and water plants can grow.

WHAT IS A YUCCA PLANT?

Yucca plants are succulents. This means that they are adapted to very dry conditions and can store water in their leaves. Other succulents are cacti, aloes, and agaves. Some species make popular house plants because they are easy to keep.

WHAT IS A JOSHUA TREE?

The Joshua tree grows in the Mojave Desert, California. It grows only about 4 inches a year. The fibers inside the tree's leaves can be used to make paper.

HOW BIG IS THE LARGEST CACTUS?

The largest of all cacti is the saguaro, or giant cactus, of the southwestern United States and Mexico. A 125-year-old saguaro can measure up to 50 feet tall and weigh as much as 6 tons.

JOSHUA TREE

Each of the tree's long and spiky leaves can survive for up to 20 years.

SAGUARO CACTUS

Cacti grow slowly in the dry desert. It may take 75 years to grow one side arm.

More desert plants >

Desert plants have adapted to dry conditions in a variety of ways. As well as the ability to store water, some plants have very long roots to search out underground water. Others can lie dormant, waiting for rain to grow.

DESERT BLOOMS •

The North American deserts can flower after rainfall.

> HOW DO DESERT FLOWERS SURVIVE DROUGHTS?

Many desert flowers live for only a short time, but survive as seeds in the desert soil. When the next rains fall, they trigger the seeds to germinate.

WHAT ARE LIVING STONES?

Living stones are special desert plants from southern Africa. They have swollen leaves and grow low down among the sand and gravel of the desert surface, looking very much like small pebbles or rocks. It is only when they flower that they reveal their true nature.

➤ HOW DO "RESURRECTION" PLANTS SURVIVE DROUGHTS?

When conditions get very dry, the leaves of these plants shrivel up and turn brown. This cuts down the loss of water. When it rains, they turn green again.

➤ WHAT IS A PRICKLY PEAR?

A prickly pear is a type of cactus. The fruits of prickly pears are commonly called cactus figs and are tasty to eat, as long as their small spines are removed.

➤ HOW DEEP DO THE ROOTS OF DESERT PLANTS GO?

Some desert plants have very long roots that can tap into deep underground water sources. Mesquite roots often grow as deep as 65 feet in search of water.

WELWITSCHIA

The plant's two leaves can grow up to 13 feet long and split into several strands.

➤ WHICH IS THE STRANGEST DESERT PLANT?

Welwitschia is probably the strangest desert plant of all. It lives for centuries, growing very slowly, and producing just two twisted leathery leaves. It lives in the coastal deserts of southwest Africa and gets its water mainly from sea fog.

Grassland >

In temperate regions—lying between the polar areas and the tropics—that have warm summers and cold winters, grassland develops in areas that do not have enough rainfall for trees and woods to grow. Many types of grasses thrive in these habitats.

> WHERE ARE GRASSLANDS FOUND?

There are grasslands in Central Asia, North America, Argentina, and southern Africa. The Asian grasslands are called the steppes, and the North American grasslands are the prairies. In Argentina, they are called pampas, and in southern Africa the veld. The steppes are the largest area, stretching from Hungary to Mongolia.

TOP QUESTION

HOW DO GRASSLAND FIRES START?

Fires can start naturally, for example when lightning strikes dead or dying grass. If a wind is blowing and the weather is dry, the sparks can quickly turn into a fire that spreads.

STEPPES

Very few trees break the monotony of the Central Asian steppes.

➤ HOW DO GRASSLAND PLANTS SURVIVE FIRE?

Some grassland plants survive fires by persisting as thickened roots, and sprouting again after the fire has passed. Others may die, but germinate again later, from seeds left behind in the soil.

➤ WHY DON'T TREES TAKE OVER THE GRASSLAND?

Trees cannot survive easily in natural grassland areas, mainly because the rainfall is too low to support their growth. But in areas where the rainfall is higher, trees will gradually invade, unless they are chopped down or eaten by grazing animals.

➤ WHICH ANIMALS LIVE ON THE PRAIRIES?

The original prairie animals include buffalo, deer, and prairie dogs. The wild buffalo once numbered about 40 million, but it was almost wiped out by settlers.

ZEBRA ON THE VELD

The zebra's stripes act as camouflage in the dappled light and shade of long grass.

➤ WHAT ARE GRASSLANDS USED FOR?

Grasslands have long been used for grazing herds of domestic animals, such as cows. But because the soils are so fertile, much of the original grasslands have now been plowed up and planted with crops, such as wheat and corn (maize).

Mountains

Conditions get harsher the higher you go up a mountain, and the plant life reflects this. Fir or pine forests on the upper slopes give way to shrubs then grassland, followed by snow and rock.

WHICH IS THE WORLD'S HIGHEST MOUNTAIN RANGE?

The Himalayas, in Asia. It contains 96 of the world's 109 peaks that are more than 24,000 feet above sea level. One of these peaks is Mount Everest, the world's highest mountain.

TOP QUESTION

WHAT IS THE TIMBERLINE?

Trees cannot grow all the way up a mountain, and the highest level for them is known as the timberline. This varies according to the local climate of the region, but is about 6,000 feet in the European Alps. Trees at this level grow slowly and are often short.

TIMBERLINE

Trees give way to grasses and higher rocky slopes.

WHY IS IT COLDER IN THE MOUNTAINS?

The Sun heats the ground and this heat is trapped close to the ground by the Earth's atmosphere. As you go up a mountain, and rise above the zone in which the heat is held, the atmosphere becomes thinner and the air gets colder. It falls about 1°F for every 250 feet you ascend in height.

WHAT ARE CONIFEROUS FORESTS?

Coniferous forests often grow on mountain slopes, as well as in many other regions. Coniferous trees are conifers, such as pines and firs. These trees are evergreen, which means they do not lose their leaves in winter. The trees cope well with weather extremes, such as cold and drought.

WHY IS IT DAMAGING TO CUT DOWN MOUNTAIN FORESTS?

On mountain slopes, forests do more than provide homes and food for animals. Tree roots anchor the soil, preventing it from being washed away by rain running down the slopes. Without trees to prevent them, dangerous landslides can occur.

HOW DO PLANT-EATING ANIMALS FIND FOOD IN THE MOUNTAINS?

Many mountain mammals burrow under the snow and continue to feed on mountain plants even at high altitudes. Others, such as marmots, store fat in their bodies and hibernate during the winter.

MOUNT EVEREST

The mountain's peak, at 29,050 feet, is bare of plants. Flowering plants grow up to 20,000 feet.

MARMOT

Marmots eat mountain grasses, berries, mosses, roots, and flowers.

Mountain plants >

On mountainsides, plants must survive colder and windier weather than on the valley floor below. They must grow in thinner soil and on uneven or rocky ground. Yet many plants thrive in these exposed conditions.

> WHY DO DIFFERENT PLANTS GROW ON DIFFERENT SIDES OF A MOUNTAIN?

Different sides of a mountain have different climates, or average weather conditions. On the south side (or north side in the southern hemisphere), there is more sunshine and conditions are warmer, while on the other side, the snow stays on the ground much longer.

ALPINE MEADOW

Dandelions and cuckoo flowers grow in grassland high in the European Alps.

> HOW DO PLANTS SURVIVE THE COLD?

Some plants grow close to the ground in pillowlike shapes, which keeps them out of the wind. Some have thick, waxy, or hairy leaves to help insulate them from the cold.

EDELWEISS

Edelweiss is a European mountain plant that thrives on rocky slopes.

❯ HOW DO PLANTS SURVIVE THE SNOW AND ICE?

Few plants can survive being completely frozen, but many can thrive under the snow. Snow acts like a blanket to keep the freezing ice and wind at bay, and saves the plants from being killed. Alpine grasses stay alive and green under the snow, ready to grow again as soon as it melts.

❯ WHY ARE ALPINE PLANTS POPULAR IN GARDENS?

Alpine plants are those that survive above the timberline. Many are popular because they have bright flowers and tend to grow well in poor conditions.

❯ HOW DO SOME MOUNTAIN PLANTS REPRODUCE WITHOUT FLOWERS?

Many mountain plants have dispensed with flowers because of the lack of insects to pollinate them. Instead, for example, some grasses grow miniature plants where the flowers should be. These drop off and grow into new plants.

GENTIAN

Many mountain plants, such as this vivid blue gentian, have showy flowers to attract insects.

❯ HOW DO MOUNTAIN PLANTS ATTRACT POLLINATORS?

Many mountain plants have large, colorful flowers to attract the few insects that live there. Some, such as mountain avens, track the sun to warm their flowers, which encourages insects to sunbathe there.

Tundra ›

Tundra is an area where the temperatures are too cold for trees to grow. Tundra normally occurs close to the polar regions. The dominant plants are grasses, mosses, lichens, and shrubs, such as heathers.

› WHERE IS THE TUNDRA?

Tundra lies north of the coniferous forest belt, in a band following the Arctic Circle. It covers about 10 million square miles, from Alaska, across Canada, Greenland, Iceland, and Scandinavia into Siberia. Only a small area of the Antarctic has similar conditions, on the northern tip nearest to South America. Most of Antarctica is covered with snow and ice all year.

WHAT IS THE MOST NORTHERLY FLOWER?

The Arctic poppy has been found growing farther north than any other flower, at 83°N, or on a level with the north of Greenland.

SIBERIAN TUNDRA

The snow melts in summer, leaving behind marshy puddles.

➤ WHAT IS PERMAFROST?

Even where the surface soil in the Arctic thaws in the summer, farther down it is permanently frozen. This icy layer is known as the permafrost.

➤ WHY ARE MANY ARCTIC SHRUBS EVERGREEN?

Many Arctic shrubs keep some of their leaves throughout the winter. Leaves formed in late summer stay on the plant, often protected by dead leaves formed earlier. As soon as spring returns, the green leaves begin to photosynthesize, losing no time to make their food during the short summer months.

➤ WHAT PLANTS DO CARIBOU EAT?

Caribou survive the Arctic winter by foraging for food. They dig beneath the snow with their hooves and antlers, seeking out mosses and grasses.

➤ WHY ARE MANY TUNDRA FLOWERS WHITE OR YELLOW?

Most tundra flowers are pollinated by insects. However, there are relatively few bees this far north, and the main pollinators are flies. Flies cannot distinguish colors like bees can, so the flowers do not need to be so colorful.

CARIBOU

The caribou, also known as the reindeer, is common in tundra regions.

Temperate forest →

There are two main types of forest in the world's temperate regions: the deciduous forest and the evergreen coniferous forest. Deciduous forests are characterized by trees that lose their leaves in the winter. Evergreen trees keep their leaves year-round.

❯ WHAT IS TEMPERATE DECIDUOUS FOREST LIKE IN SUMMER?

In summer, the forests hum with life—birds call from the trees and mice rustle in the undergrowth. The leaf canopy is fully developed, cutting out much of the sunlight from the forest floor. Nevertheless, shrubs, such as roses and hazel, and flowers, such as woodsorrel, grow among the trees.

❯ WHAT IS TEMPERATE DECIDUOUS FOREST LIKE IN WINTER?

In winter, the tall trees forming the woodland canopy have lost all their leaves. Most of the flowers have died back. Evergreen species, such as holly, ivy, and yew, stand out at this time of year, and provide valuable cover for forest animals.

❯ ARE TEMPERATE FORESTS QUIETER IN WINTER?

Yes! Many of the birds heard in temperate forests are summer visitors and migrate south in winter. Many chirping forest insects die or hibernate during the cold winters.

SUMMER WOODLAND

Beneath the canopy of trees, layers of shrubs and herbs grow closer to the ground.

➤ HOW ARE TEMPERATE FORESTS HARVESTED FOR WOOD?

Many forests are not natural but have been managed for centuries to provide wood. This involves removing only a portion of the tree at a time, which lets the forest regenerate. Sometimes branches are cut from trees, and the trees can then resprout from the base to provide another crop of branches later. This is called coppicing.

➤ WHAT ELSE DO WE GET FROM TEMPERATE FORESTS?

Lots of things! Charcoal is made by slowly burning certain kinds of wood. In the past, people depended upon woodland animals, such as wild boar and deer, for food and skins. Many edible fungi, including chanterelle and truffles, grow in temperate woods, while woodland brambles and wild strawberries have edible fruits.

TOP ? QUESTION

WHAT LIVES ON THE FOREST FLOOR?

Invertebrates thrive in the dead leaves and roots of the woodland floor. Beetles, wood lice (above), worms, slugs, snails, and ants, to name but a few, help break down the organic material, as well as providing food for mice and voles.

MUSHROOM

A mushroom is the fleshy body of a fungus.

Temperate forest plants >

Temperate forests are found in parts of North America, Europe, eastern Asia, South America, and Australasia. The most common plants are trees, but shrubs and low-growing plants also thrive.

> WHY DO SOME TREES LOSE THEIR LEAVES IN FALL?

Deciduous trees and other plants that lose their leaves usually do so in fall, and remain bare throughout winter. In this way, they shut down their main life processes—photosynthesis and transpiration (through which water and nutrients flow through the plant)—remaining dormant until spring.

FALL LEAF

A leaf's green pigment decreases as winter nears.

> WHY DO MOST WOODLAND FLOWERS APPEAR IN SPRING?

By developing early, they can benefit from the sunlight before it is shut out by the trees. Insects, which help to pollinate flowers, may also find it easier to spot them before the rest of the vegetation grows.

> WHICH ARE THE MOST COMMON TREES?

The most common trees in deciduous forests are oaks, beeches, maples, and birches. Common coniferous trees are pines, firs, and spruces.

BLUEBELLS

Bluebells are common in European woods in spring.

> WHICH FOREST TREE CAN BE TRACKED DOWN BY ITS SOUND?

The leaves of the aspen tree move from side to side in the wind and rustle against each other, even in the lightest breeze. So an expert listener can easily track down an aspen.

> WHICH CONIFER IS DECIDUOUS?

Larch is a coniferous tree—it bears cones and has needlelike leaves. But unlike most conifers, larch loses its leaves all at once, in fall, so it is also deciduous. In fact, there are also broad-leaved trees that are evergreen, such as the oaks of the Mediterranean regions.

> HOW OLD CAN FOREST TREES GET?

Many forest trees reach a great age, notably oaks, which live between 200 and 400 years. Most elms live to about 150 years of age.

LARCH CONE

When fertilized by pollen, a cone produces seeds.

Rain forest >

Tropical rain forests occur in the earth's hotter regions where rainfall is very high. The rain forests help preserve the planet's atmosphere by releasing huge quantities of water vapor and oxygen and absorbing carbon dioxide.

> HOW MUCH RAIN FALLS IN THE RAIN FOREST?

The tropical rain forests are warm and wet. In many, the rainfall is more than 6 feet per year. It may rain at any time of the day, but there are often storms in the afternoon.

> WHERE ARE THE RAIN FORESTS?

The world's largest rainforest is around Brazil's Amazon River and the foothills of the Andes Mountains. The world's main areas of tropical rain forest are in South and Central America, West and Central Africa, Southeast Asia, and north Australia.

RAIN FOREST

Just one acre of tropical rain forest can contain 200 species of trees.

WHAT DO WE GET FROM RAIN FORESTS?

We get many things from rain forests, including wood, Brazil nuts, fruit (such as bananas and mangoes), rubber, rattan (a kind of palm from which furniture is made), cosmetics, and medicines.

❯ WHY ARE RAIN FORESTS BEING CUT DOWN?

Many rain forests are destroyed so the land can be used for crops, or for grazing. Tropical forest soils are fertile, and many crops, such as cocoa and sugar cane, can be grown after the trees have been felled. However, the fertility of the soil is short-lived.

RAIN FOREST FRUIT

Pineapple and urucum (above right) grow in tropical forests.

❯ HOW FAST ARE RAIN FORESTS BEING DESTROYED?

Every year an area of rain forest the size of Wisconsin is lost. When the forest is cleared, the fertile topsoil is soon washed away by tropical rainstorms, making the ground useless for crops.

❯ ARE RAIN FORESTS VITAL?

Yes! Rain forests are home to two-thirds of the world's animal and plant species. And without rain forests to regulate the Earth's atmosphere, climate change would speed up.

Rain forest plants >

The rain forest is in four basic layers. At the top are the very tallest trees. Below is the canopy, a dense cover of foliage made by the bulk of the trees. The understory is the layer of shrubs, while the forest floor below is dimly lit and relatively bare of plants.

> HOW TALL ARE THE BIGGEST RAIN FOREST TREES?

The main canopy of the rain forest develops at around 100 feet, with occasional taller trees (known as emergents) rising above to about 160 feet or more.

> WHAT STOPS THE TALL TREES FROM BEING BLOWN OVER?

Many of the taller forest trees have special supporting flanges near the base of their trunks, called stilts or buttresses. These make the tree less liable to be pushed over in a storm.

BROMELIAD

The plant's colored leaves form a rosette to trap vital water.

TOP QUESTION

WHICH PLANTS CAN TRAP THEIR OWN RAIN WATER?

It rains very often in the tropical rain forest, and many plants trap the water before it reaches the ground. Bromeliads have special leaves that form a waterproof cup for this purpose.

LIANA SWING

An orang-utan uses a liana as a swing in Borneo, Southeast Asia.

➤ WHAT IS AN AIR PLANT?

An air plant grows without anchoring itself to the ground. Air plants are common in some tropical forests. They get the moisture they need directly from the damp air.

➤ WHAT ARE LIANAS?

Lianas, or lianes, are plants that clamber over and dangle from rain-forest trees. They grow very long, and animals, such as monkeys and squirrels use lianas to help them move through the branches.

ORCHID

Many orchids are air plants, with roots that cling onto other plants for support.

➤ WHAT'S A STRANGLER FIG?

The strangler starts out as a seed high in a tree, carried there by a monkey or bird that has eaten the fig's fruit. The seedling sends down long roots to the ground, from where it starts to surround the host tree, slowly suffocating it.

Wetland

Wetlands include swamps, bogs, and marshes. Wetland plants are adapted to living in water-soaked soil. Bulrushes, water lilies, and mangroves are just some of the common wetland species.

> WHY DO MOST WATER PLANTS GROW ONLY IN SHALLOW WATER?

Most plants need to root themselves in the soil, even if they live mainly submerged in the water. In deep water, there is not enough sunlight for plants to grow successfully.

> HOW ARE WETLANDS DAMAGED?

When soil is drained, or too much water is pumped from the land nearby, wetlands suffer as the water table is lowered. They are also easily damaged by pollution. Chemicals released from factories find their way into streams, upsetting the natural balance.

> WHAT IS THE WATER HYACINTH?

Water hyacinth is a floating plant with beautiful mauve flowers. However, it is also a fast-growing weed and can spread rapidly to choke waterways.

WATER HYACINTH

Water hyacinths flourish on Lake Naivasha in Kenya, eastern Africa.

> HOW DO WATER PLANTS GET THEIR FLOWERS POLLINATED?

Most water plants hold their flowers above the water for pollination by the wind or by insects. Some, such as the water starwort, have water-resistant floating pollen that drifts to the female flowers.

DRAGONFLY

Dragonflies live around wetlands because they lay eggs in or near water.

> WHAT FOOD PLANTS COME FROM WETLANDS?

The most important wetland crop is rice, which is grown in many parts of the world, notably India and China. It grows best in flooded fields called paddies. Another aquatic grass crop is Canadian wild rice, a traditional food of Native Americans, and now a popular specialty.

HOW DO WATER PLANTS STAY AFLOAT?

Some water plants stay afloat because their tissues contain chambers of air, making their stems and leaves buoyant. Others, such as water lilies, have flat, rounded leaves that sit boatlike on the water's surface. They may also have waxy leaves, which repel the water and help to keep the leaves afloat, or up-curved rims on the leaves.

Life in the sea

Shape and color ➤

An amazing range of animals lives in the world's seas and oceans. Sea creatures include fish, reptiles (such as sea turtles), mammals (such as whales and dolphins), and invertebrates (animals without a backbone) from jellyfish to lobsters. All sea creatures have shapes that allow them to move easily through the water. In many cases, their colors act as vital camouflage.

➤ **WHY DO SOME FISH HAVE BRIGHT COLORS?**

Many fish that live in tropical seas are brightly colored or boldly patterned. This coloring helps them to hide among brightly colored coral. But in the breeding season, when these fish are seeking mates, they swim out into the open and become very obvious.

TANGS

Shoals of yellow tangs are found swimming among tropical coral reefs.

CARPET SHARK

Carpet sharks use camouflage to ambush their prey on the seabed.

❯ HOW DOES THE CARPET SHARK HIDE?

Many sea creatures have bodies with colors, shapes, and patterns that blend in with their surroundings. This camouflage, or natural disguise, helps them to hide from enemies or sneak up on their prey. The pale, blotchy colors of carpet sharks help hide them from their prey—small fish and crabs—as they lie motionless on the seabed.

❯ WHAT'S THE WORLD'S LONGEST FISH?

Oarfish are giant, eel-shape fish that regularly grow over 20 feet long. Individuals as large as 55 feet long have been recorded. Legends of sea serpents may have been inspired by glimpses of these amazing creatures.

❯ HOW DO FISH HIDE IN THE OPEN SEA?

Herring, mackerel, and many other fish that swim near the surface of the great oceans have dark backs and pale bellies. This coloring, called countershading, works to cancel out the effect of sunlight shining on their bodies from above, and so helps these fish to hide, even in open water.

TOP ? QUESTION

WHAT CREATURES PLANT A GARDEN ON THEIR BACKS?

Spider crabs (right) make their own disguises from materials they find around them. They clip living sponges or fronds of seaweed with their strong pincers, and plant them on their backs. When the seaweed dies, they replace it with more!

Swimming and movement →

Sea creatures move through the water in many different ways—from sperm whales that dive to depths of 1,500 feet to fish that can fly through the air. Most fish and marine mammals have sleek, streamlined bodies that allow them to slip through the water. Some invertebrates make use of jet propulsion by shooting out a stream of water behind themselves. Many marine reptiles use strong flippers to paddle through the water.

> HOW DO FISH SWIM?

Most fish swim by arching their bodies and swishing their tails from side to side. The fish's body and tail push against the water to propel it forward. The chest, back, and belly fins help with steering and braking. A gas-filled organ called the swim bladder keeps the fish buoyant in the water.

> WHICH FISH FLIES UNDERWATER?

Rays are flattened fish that live near the seabed. They swim along by flapping their wide, flat chest fins like wings, so they look as if they are flying underwater.

FINS
Rays use their immense chest fins as wings, flapping gracefully through the water.

MANTA RAY
The manta ray is the largest of the rays and can measure more than 25 feet across. It lives in tropical waters.

? TOP QUESTION

WHICH FISH FLIES THROUGH THE AIR?

Flying fish (right) take to the air to escape from hungry predators. The flying fish gets up speed, then leaps right out of the water. In the air, it spreads its chest fins so they act like wings, sometimes keeping the fish airborne for over 330 feet.

❯ HOW DO JELLYFISH GET AROUND?

Jellyfish are soft creatures with bodies shaped like bells or saucers. To get around, they contract their baglike bodies, so water shoots out behind, pushing the creature along.

❯ WHICH FISH CAN WALK ON LAND?

Mudskippers are fish that live in swamps and muddy estuaries on tropical coasts. They come right out of the water and scurry around on land, using their muscular chest fins as crutches.

MUDSKIPPER

Mudskippers are able to leave the water for long periods, as long as they keep themselves damp.

The diets of sea animals range from plants and tiny drifting creatures called plankton to absolutely anything that moves in the water. Some extraordinary methods are used by sea creatures to hunt down and kill their prey, from ambush attacks to electric shocks.

THE CLEANER

The cleaner wrasse feeds on parasites in the mouths and on the bodies of larger fish.

THE CUSTOMER

Cleaner wrasses are rarely eaten by predators because they are more valuable kept alive.

> WHICH FISH RUNS A CLEANING SERVICE?

Small fish called cleaner wrasse feed on parasites that infest larger fish. The big fish welcome this cleaning service, so do not harm the wrasse, even when it swims right inside a big fish's mouth to clean. Sometimes lines of fish form at the wrasse's cleaning station, patiently waiting their turn for a "wash and brushup."

> WHICH FISH HAS A FISHING ROD?

The anglerfish has a built-in fishing rod on its head—a long spine with a lobe on the end that looks like a worm. The angler lurks on the seabed. When a small crab comes up to eat the "worm," the anglerfish grabs its prey in its enormous mouth.

ANGLERFISH

A deep-sea anglerfish waits for its prey with its frondy lure.

> HOW DO DEEP-SEA CREATURES LIGHT UP THE DARK?

As many as 1,000 different fish make light in the deep oceans. Some have luminous bacteria living under their skin. Others have special light-producing organs, or can cause a chemical reaction that gives off light.

> HOW DOES THE ANEMONE CATCH ITS DINNER?

Sea anemones are invertebrates that are armed with a crown of stinging tentacles. When small fish brush against them, the stings fire and release a paralyzing poison. The tentacles then push the weakened prey into the anemone's mouth.

> WHICH FISH HAS A SECRET WEAPON?

The torpedo ray. It can generate electricity using special muscles in its head. The ray lurks on the seabed, waiting for small fish to pounce on. It wraps its fins around its victims and blasts them with a charge of 200 volts.

TORPEDO RAY

The torpedo ray uses electric current to stun its prey.

Escape tactics →

In the battle for survival in our oceans and seas, marine creatures have developed many different tactics for escaping capture by their predators. Fish may swim in large shoals to give them safety in numbers. Pincers, stings, clouds of ink, and sharp spines are just some of the other defenses used by creatures around the world.

CUTTLEFISH

The cuttlefish, which is actually an invertebrate rather than a fish, can squirt out ink.

❯ WHICH CREATURE CAN GROW NEW ARMS?

The starfish is an invertebrate that usually has five arms, although some species have a greater number. If a hungry predator bites off one of its arms, the starfish can grow a new one to replace it.

❯ WHICH FISH BLOWS ITSELF UP INTO A PRICKLY BALL TO DETER ENEMIES?

The porcupine fish is named for the sharp spines, like a porcupine's, on its body. Usually the spines lie flat against the fish's body, but if danger threatens, it can raise them. If an enemy comes too close, the fish takes in water so that its body swells to twice its normal size. It becomes a prickly ball too uncomfortable for predators to swallow.

LUZON STARFISH

A six-arm luzon starfish is regrowing one of its limbs.

➤ WHICH CREATURE SQUIRTS INK AT ITS ENEMIES?

Cuttlefish are relatives of squid and octopus. Like their cousins, they can produce a cloud of ink to confuse their enemies. The cuttlefish jets away under cover of this smokescreen.

➤ WHAT IS SLIMY AND HIDES IN ANEMONES?

Clownfish hide from their enemies among the stinging tentacles of sea anemones. The tentacles do not harm the clownfish because its body is covered with a thick layer of slimy mucus, but no predator dares to come close!

TOP QUESTION ?

WHAT CREATURE GIVES A NASTY NIP?

Crabs and their relatives, lobsters, belong to a group of invertebrates called crustaceans. The crab's soft body parts are protected by a hard outer shell that forms a suit of armor. The creature is also armed with claws that can give a nasty nip if an enemy comes too close.

DECAPOD

Crabs are decapods, meaning that they have ten legs. The front pair is armed with claws.

CRAB SHELL

Like all crustaceans, a crab is protected by a hard outer shell, known as an exoskeleton, or external skeleton.

Deadly and poisonous >

More than 50 different kinds of poisonous fish lurk in the world's oceans. Some are armed with venomous spines, while others have poisonous flesh. Some invertebrates and reptiles also use poison to keep predators away or to stun their prey. Many poisonous animals are brightly colored to act as a warning to predators.

> WHICH IS THE WORLD'S MOST POISONOUS REPTILE?

The bite of the yellow-bellied sea snake is 50 times more powerful than that of the dreaded king cobra. Its bold yellow-and-black colors warn of danger.

> WHICH OCTOPUS IS DEADLY POISONOUS?

The bite of the blue-ringed octopus is deadly poisonous. Normally, the creature's skin is sandy-colored, which helps it blend in with the seabed. But when the octopus is alarmed and ready to bite, blue rings appear all over its body.

WARNING!

The spots of the blue-ringed octopus warn predators to keep clear.

> WHICH "STONE" CAN KILL?

The stonefish of Australian waters is one of the deadliest sea creatures. If a person steps on the fish, its spines release a poison that causes agonizing pain. The victim may die of shock, heart failure, or breathing problems.

STINGRAY

The stinging barb at the end of the tail can be up to 15 inches long.

> **HOW DOES A JELLYFISH STING?**

The long tentacles of jellyfish are armed with thousands of stinging cells. When a fish brushes against a tentacle, the barbs fire and release a paralyzing poison.

> **WHAT IS THE STINGRAY'S SECRET WEAPON?**

Stingrays live and hunt on the ocean bottom. Their long, thin tails are armed with barbs that can inject a painful poison.

TOP ? QUESTION

WHICH POISONOUS FISH DO PEOPLE EAT?

The entrails of the pufferfish contain a powerful poison. Yet other parts of the fish taste delicious! In Japan, the fish is served as a delicacy called *fugu*. Japanese chefs are trained to remove all traces of the poisonous organs.

PUFFERFISH

The organs of the starry pufferfish contain a poison deadly to humans.

Courting and breeding >

When it is time to breed, male and female sea creatures must attract each other, using methods from bright colors to beautiful songs. Most fish and marine reptiles and invertebrates lay eggs, but some give birth to live young.

> HOW DO HUMPBACK WHALES GO COURTING?

Humpback whales make many different sounds, including clicks, squeaks, moans, and roars. To attract a partner, the male humpback sings a "song" made up of different noises. Each male sings a different tune, lasting for hours.

> WHAT MAKES A FIDDLER CRAB SEXY?

Male fiddler crabs have a built-in "sex symbol"— one claw that is much bigger than the other. On the seashore, the males attract attention by waving their giant claws.

> HOW DOES THE DAMSEL FISH LOOK AFTER ITS EGGS?

Most fish take little care of their eggs—they just spawn (lay and fertilize their eggs) and swim away without a backward glance. Damsel fish are one of the exceptions. The females glue their eggs carefully to rocks. The males are caring fathers. They guard and check the eggs until they hatch, and shoo off any other fish that approach to eat them.

FIDDLER CRAB

Female fiddler crabs choose the males with the biggest claws (left).

WHICH SEA CREATURE COMES ASHORE TO BREED?

Green turtles spend their lives at sea, but come on land to breed. The female swims ashore and digs a hole in a beach (left) to lay her eggs. When the baby turtles hatch, they dig themselves out of the sand, then dash down to the water.

SEA HORSES

Male and female sea horses court each other for several days in the breeding season. They may even change color and hold each other's tails.

❯ WHICH MALE FISH GETS PREGNANT?

Sea horses have extraordinary breeding habits. The female lays her eggs in a little pouch on the male sea horse's belly. The eggs develop in the safety of the pouch. Around a month later, an amazing sight occurs, as the male "gives birth" to hundreds of tiny sea horses.

Young sea creatures ➤

BLUE WHALE CALF

A blue whale calf feeds on its mother's milk for six months after it is born. It forms a close bond with its mother, swimming near to her side.

Most fish species leave their young to look after themselves. For this reason, most fish produce many eggs to make sure that some survive. In contrast, marine mammals give birth to a small number of live young, with whom they can form strong bonds.

➤ WHICH CREATURE HAS THE LARGEST BABY?

Female blue whales, the largest whales, also bear the biggest babies. A newborn blue whale calf measures 23 feet long and may weigh 2.5 tons—as much as a full-grown elephant! The thirsty baby drinks huge quantities of its mother's milk and puts on weight fast. At six months old, it may be as much as 52 feet long.

➤ HOW DO YOUNG SEA OTTERS LEARN THEIR SKILLS?

Sea otters (mother and pup seen on the left) often learn through play. Mother otters sometimes bring their young an injured fish to play with. As the pups take turns to catch their weakened prey, they learn hunting skills that will be vital to them later.

MOTHER BLUE WHALE

Female blue whales give birth to one calf about every two to three years, after a pregnancy of 10 to 12 months.

TOP ? QUESTION

WHICH MOTHER HAS A MOUTHFUL OF BABIES?

Few fish look after their babies, but fish known as mouthbreeders are the exception. Mouthbreeders, such as some species of cichlids, protect their young by hiding them in their mouths! The babies swim in a cloud near their mother's head. When danger threatens, they scoot back inside her mouth (right).

❯ WHICH YOUNG FISH HAS A LONG WAY TO TRAVEL?

Young salmon hatch out and grow in shallow streams inland. After several years, they swim downriver to the sea and spend their adult lives in the ocean. To breed, they fight their way back upriver to lay eggs (spawn) in the same stream where they hatched out.

❯ WHICH FISH EATS ITS BROTHERS AND SISTERS?

Sand tiger shark eggs hatch out inside their mother's body. The tiny embryo sharks feed on one another until only one big, strong baby is left, ready to be born.

Coral reef →

Coral reefs are made of tiny creatures called polyps that live in colonies, or groups, in tropical seas. The world's reefs support a huge range of ocean life, from more than 4,000 species of colorful fish to extraordinary invertebrates.

❯ WHAT IS A LEAFY SEA DRAGON?

The leafy sea dragon is related to the sea horses and lives in warm Australian water. This creature is a master of disguise. Its body is covered with long, trailing flaps of skin that look like strands of seaweed.

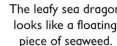

SEA DRAGON

The leafy sea dragon looks like a floating piece of seaweed.

❯ WHAT IS CORAL MADE OF?

The polyps that form coral reefs are shaped like little sea anemones, but have a hard, chalky cup-shape shell to protect their bodies. When they die, the shells remain and new polyps grow on top of them. Over time, billions of shells build up to form a coral reef.

RED SEA REEF

The Red Sea Reef is located off the coasts of Israel, Egypt, and Saudi Arabia.

➤ WHERE IS THE WORLD'S LARGEST CORAL REEF?

The Great Barrier Reef off the northeastern coast of Australia is the world's largest coral reef. Stretching for 1,250 miles, it is the largest structure made by living creatures. The reef is home to many spectacular animals, including 1,500 different kinds of fish.

➤ WHAT ARE DEAD MAN'S FINGERS?

Dead man's fingers is a species of soft coral that grows on rocks. Each coral colony is made up of thousands of polyps that form a fleshy mass like a rubbery hand. When a piece of this coral washes up on the seashore, it may frighten the swimmers!

WHAT CLAMS UP IN A HURRY?

Giant clams live on the Great Barrier Reef. Their huge, hinged shells measure up to 5 feet wide and weigh 550 pounds. The giant clam generally has its shell open so it can feed, but if danger threatens, it can slam the two halves shut.

REEF FISH

The fish species that inhabit reefs are often as colorful as the reefs themselves.

GIANT CLAM

Giant clams are endangered due to the loss of their habitat and the sale of their beautiful shells for use as ornaments.

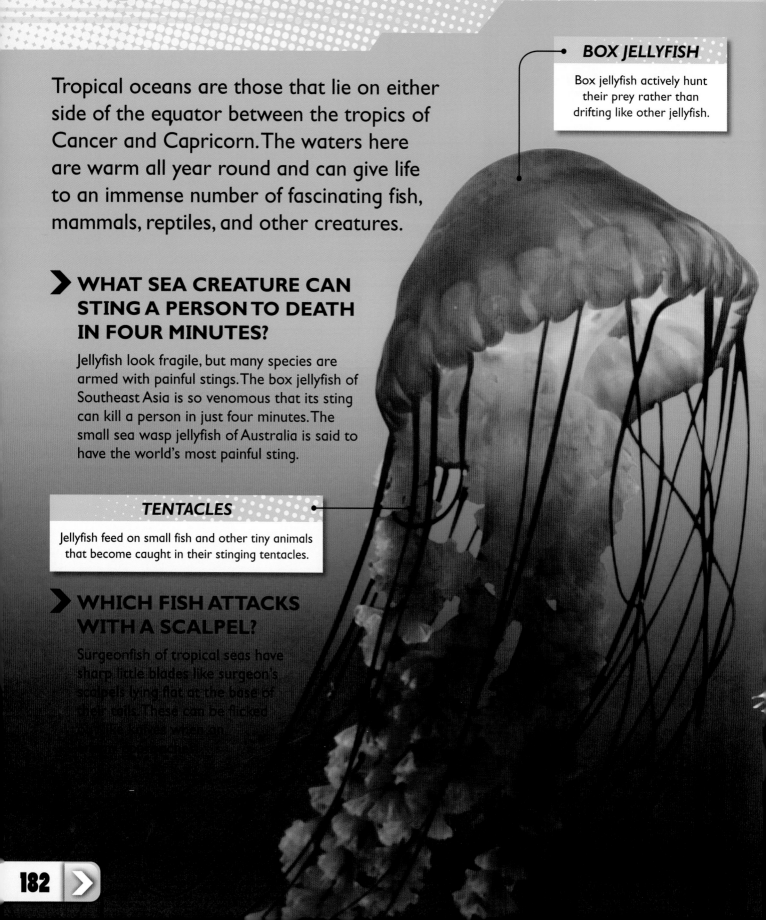

Tropical oceans →

Tropical oceans are those that lie on either side of the equator between the tropics of Cancer and Capricorn. The waters here are warm all year round and can give life to an immense number of fascinating fish, mammals, reptiles, and other creatures.

❯ WHAT SEA CREATURE CAN STING A PERSON TO DEATH IN FOUR MINUTES?

Jellyfish look fragile, but many species are armed with painful stings. The box jellyfish of Southeast Asia is so venomous that its sting can kill a person in just four minutes. The small sea wasp jellyfish of Australia is said to have the world's most painful sting.

TENTACLES

Jellyfish feed on small fish and other tiny animals that become caught in their stinging tentacles.

❯ WHICH FISH ATTACKS WITH A SCALPEL?

Surgeonfish of tropical seas have sharp little blades like surgeon's scalpels lying flat at the base of their tails. These can be flicked

BOX JELLYFISH

Box jellyfish actively hunt their prey rather than drifting like other jellyfish.

ARE MERMAIDS REAL?

In bygone times, sailors sometimes reported seeing mermaids—creatures with the head and body of a woman and a fish's tail. Experts believe these stories may have been inspired by dugongs (right), sea mammals with rounded faces, which often hold their bodies upright in the water. Dugongs live in the tropical Indian and Pacific oceans.

WHICH DEADLY FISH LOOKS LIKE A TOAD?

The toadfish is a poisonous fish that dwells on the seabed in warm oceans. With its bulging eyes, large mouth, and blotchy skin, the fish is well named, since it looks just like a toad.

WHICH FISH HAS DEVIL'S HORNS?

The manta ray, or devilfish, has two fins that curve forward from its head like devil's horns. The ray uses its "horns" to scoop food into its mouth as it swims along the seabed.

WHY ARE LIONFISH BRIGHTLY COLORED?

The lionfish is a beautiful but deadly fish of tropical waters. Its long, graceful spines contain a lethal poison. The lionfish drifts lazily though the water with its orange-striped coloring, yet few enemies dare to approach it. The fish's bright colors warn that it is poisonous. They are a signal known and recognized throughout the animal world.

LIONFISH

Also known as the dragonfish or scorpionfish, the lionfish's striped colors warn enemies to keep away.

Shore and seabed >

Creatures that live on the ocean floor or the shore have developed different survival strategies than those that live in the open oceans. Shore dwellers must cope with the constant breaking of waves and changes in water level. Many animals that live on the seabed feed on feces and dead animals and plants.

> WHAT LINES UP FOR ITS WINTER VACATION?

Spiny lobsters live mainly solitary lives. But each year in fall they gather to move to deeper waters where they will be safe from violent storms. The lobsters form a long line and march off along the seabed.

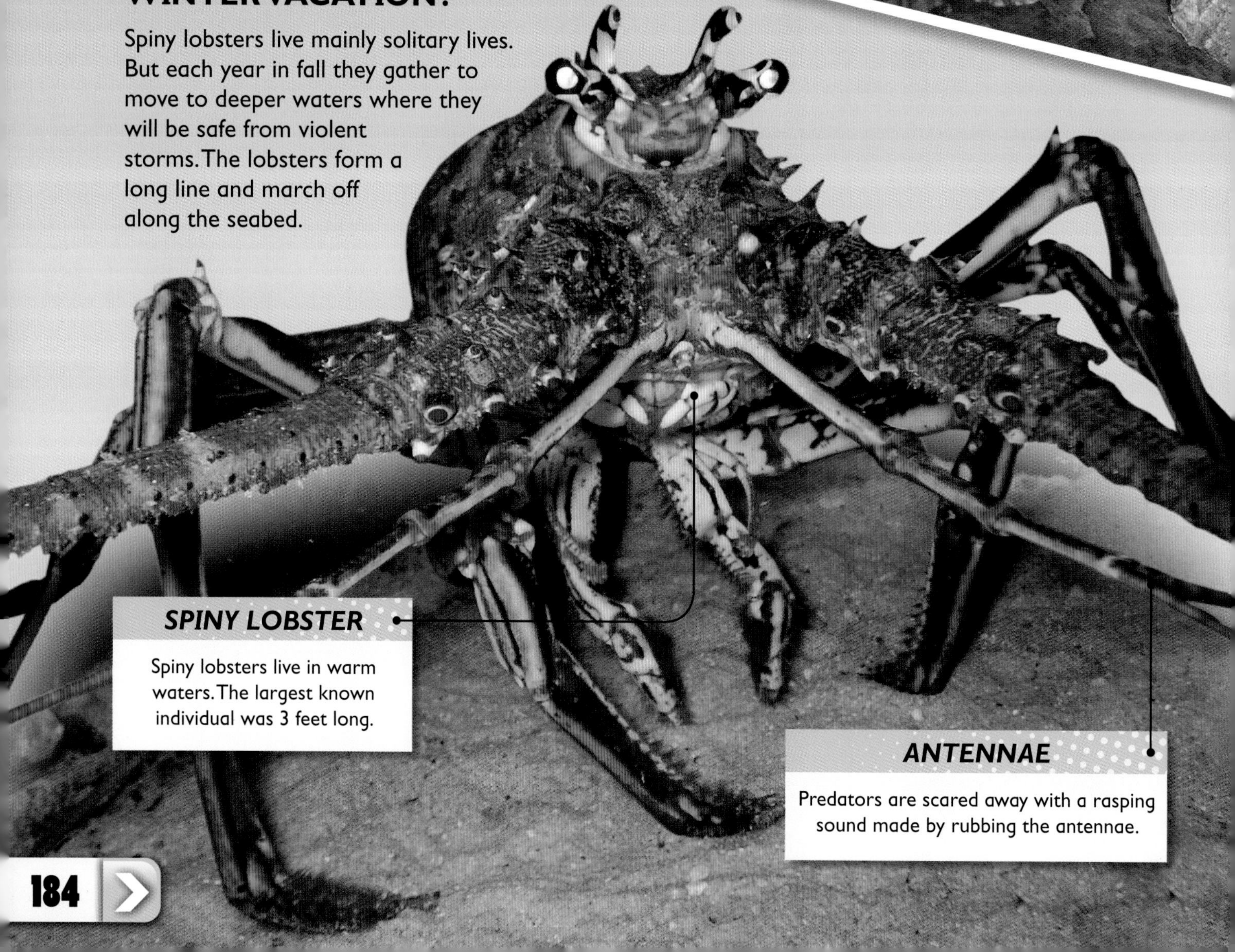

SPINY LOBSTER

Spiny lobsters live in warm waters. The largest known individual was 3 feet long.

ANTENNAE

Predators are scared away with a rasping sound made by rubbing the antennae.

TOP QUESTION ?

HOW DOES A LIMPET GRIP ITS ROCK?

The limpet (left) clamps its muscular foot onto a seashore rock and grips by suction. Even the pounding waves cannot dislodge it. Its hold is so tight that it can be pried away only if an enemy attacks without warning.

➤ WHY DO CRABS WALK SIDEWAYS?

Crabs scuttle sideways along the shore and seabed. The sideways movement helps to prevent them from tripping over their own legs! Large species of crab move only slowly, but small ghost crabs can scurry along the shore at a fast clip.

➤ WHAT BURIES ITSELF IN THE SAND?

Many creatures that dwell on the ocean bottom escape from their enemies by burying themselves in the sand or mud. Crabs dig down and lie low with just their sensitive antennae showing. Weeverfish, which hide in the same way, have eyes on top of their heads.

➤ WHICH CREATURE HAS FIVE SETS OF JAWS?

Underneath its round, spiny body, the sea urchin has a mouth with five sets of jaws. It feeds by crawling along the seabed, scraping seaweed and tiny creatures from the rocks.

SEA URCHIN

The spiny sea urchin moves along the seabed using its hundreds of tiny, adhesive tube feet, which work by suction.

Scary sharks >

Sharks are a type of fish with a streamlined body. There are about 380 different species of shark. Only a few species are fierce predators that hunt prey, such as seals, squid, and penguins. Most sharks, such as basking sharks, feed on tiny creatures that they filter from the water using their strainer-like mouths.

> WHICH IS THE WORLD'S MOST DEADLY SHARK?

The great white shark is the world's most feared sea creature. It is responsible for more attacks on humans than any other shark. Great whites grow to 23 feet long. Tiger and bull sharks are also known as killers.

REEF SHARK

A reef shark feeds on fish, crabs, squid, and cuttlefish as it coasts through tropical waters.

TOP QUESTION ?

WHAT HAS UP TO 3,000 TEETH?

Hunting sharks have teeth with jagged edges like a saw. A shark may have as many as 3,000 teeth in its mouth, arranged in up to 20 rows, but only the teeth on the outer edge of the jaw are used for biting. The inner teeth move outward to replace teeth when they break.

> WHAT WOULD SINK IF IT DID NOT SWIM?

Most fish have a special organ called a swim bladder that helps them to float. Sharks have no swim bladder, so they must keep swimming to avoid sinking. Moving forward also keeps a supply of oxygen-rich seawater flowing over the shark's gills, which helps it to breathe.

➤ WHICH SHARK HAS A HEAD LIKE A HAMMER?

The hammerhead shark (right) is named for its peculiar head, shaped like a giant letter T. The shark's eyes and nostrils are on the ends of its "hammer." As it moves along the seabed, it swings its head from side to side. Some scientists believe that the widely spaced eyes and nostrils help the hammerhead home in on its prey.

➤ HOW DO SHARKS TRACK PREY?

Sharks have many senses that help with hunting. An excellent sense of smell allows the shark to detect tiny amounts of blood in the water and track down distant wounded animals. A special sense called "distant touch" helps it to pick up vibrations caused by swimming creatures. At closer range, sensory pores on the shark's snout detect tiny electrical signals given off by prey animals' muscles. Sight and hearing also help the shark.

KILLING MACHINE

The great white shark has a sleek body and a strong tail and fins that allow it to swim at up to 15 miles an hour.

GREAT WHITE TEETH

Great whites have such powerful jaws that they can sever a human arm or leg in a single bite.

Sea mammals >

There are about 120 marine mammals that live in the oceans or depend on them for food. Sea mammals include whales, dolphins, porpoises, manatees, dugongs, seals, walruses, and sea otters. Like all mammals, they breathe oxygen and so must come to the surface to breathe. Mammals give birth to live young, which are fed on their mother's milk.

> WHICH CREATURE HOLDS THE RECORD FOR LONG-DISTANCE TRAVEL?

Gray whales are the champion travelers of the oceans. Each year, they journey from their breeding grounds in the tropics to feeding grounds in the Arctic, and back again—a round trip of up to 12,500 miles.

> WHY DO WHALES AND DOLPHINS COME TO THE SURFACE?

With their streamlined shapes, whales and dolphins look a lot like fish, but they are really oceangoing mammals. Like all mammals, they breathe oxygen from the air. One or two nostrils called blowholes on top of the animal's head allow it to breathe without lifting its head from the water.

HUMPBACK WHALE

An adult humpback whale measures a massive 40 to 52 feet in length. Despite its size, it is an acrobatic animal, often "breaching" out of the water and slapping the surface with a splash.

FLIPPER

The humpback's very long flippers help it to steer through the water.

The sea otter (below) makes its home among the kelp weed beds of the eastern Pacific. While resting, the otter wraps seaweed fronds around its body so it does not drift away with the ocean currents.

➤ WHICH IS THE CLEVEREST SEA CREATURE?

Dolphins (above) are among the world's most intelligent creatures. Tests in aquariums show they learn to perform new tasks quickly, and can even pass on their skills by "talking" to dolphins in other tanks. Sea otters are clever too, and they are one of the few animals able to use tools. They break open the shells of crabs by smashing them against a flat rock.

➤ WHAT HUNTS BY SONAR?

Dolphins hunt with the aid of their own sonar system, called echolocation. As they swim along, they produce a stream of clicking sounds. Sound waves from the clicks bounce back when they hit an object, such as a fish. The dolphin can sense the size and direction of its prey by listening to the echoes.

Birds

Beaks, bones, wings, and feet ➤

There are around 10,000 species of bird in the world today. Scientists think that birds evolved from dinosaurs an amazing 100 million years ago. Birds have a lightweight but strong skeleton. Their front limbs have evolved into wings. Their toothless beaks are shaped—as hooks or points— to enable them to feed.

➤ WHICH BIRD HAS THE LONGEST WINGS?

The wandering albatross has a wingspan—the distance from one wingtip to the other when the wings are stretched out—of more than 10 feet. The longest ever measured was a male with a wingspan of almost 11½ feet. Females are usually smaller.

ALBATROSS WINGS

This seabird has large wings ideal for gliding over large expanses of ocean looking for fish and squid to dive for.

➤ WHY DO BIRDS' KNEES BEND BACKWARD?

They don't. What looks like the bird's knee is in fact its ankle, and below it is an extended foot bone leading to the toes. Its real knee is usually hidden by feathers.

➤ WHICH BIRDS TROT ON LILIES?

Jacanas live on ponds and lakes, walking on lily pads to catch insects that live on them. Their long toes spread their weight so that the leaves don't bend and sink.

➤ WHY DO SOME BIRDS HAVE HOOKED BEAKS?

For catching and tearing their prey. Hawks, eagles, vultures, owls, and shrikes need to be able to take a firm grip on struggling prey animals, and then pull them apart to eat them. The edges of an eagle's beak act like a pair of scissors to cut through skin and flesh. Gulls have a sharp hook at the tip of their bill to hold onto slippery fish or squid.

SHARP BEAK

An albatross's beak is large, strong, and sharp-edged for feeding on slippery fish. This bird also has a very sharp sense of smell, perfect for searching out food.

TOP QUESTION ?

WHY ARE BIRD BONES FILLED WITH AIR?

The long bones of birds are like tubes, often with crisscrossing inside, to make them strong but light. Not all birds have equally hollow bones. For example, those that dive into water, like gannets and kingfishers, have less air in their bones.

BALD EAGLE

The strong talons and sharp, hooked beak of the bald eagle help it to catch and tear apart its prey.

Flight

With some rare exceptions, most birds can fly. Flight is used for searching for food, escaping from predators, finding mates, and migration. The shape and size of a bird's wings are suited to its style of flying—whether that is gliding or hovering.

HUMMINGBIRD

Hummingbirds feed on the nectar of plants by inserting their long, straight bills right into the flower.

HOW DOES A HUMMINGBIRD HOVER?

By keeping its body nearly vertical while its wings beat forward and backward. It is actually flying upward just fast enough to balance its body weight, so that it stays still. A ruby-throated hummingbird, which weighs less than ½ ounce, has to beat its wings more than 52 times a second to hover in front of a flower.

WHICH IS THE HEAVIEST FLYING BIRD?

The Kori bustard, from eastern and southern Africa, which weighs up to 40 pounds. Because it finds flying very difficult, the Kori bustard only flies for short distances in emergencies.

WHAT KEEPS A BIRD IN THE AIR?

The shape of its wings. The upper surface of a wing is raised in a curve, so that air traveling across it has to move faster than air moving under it. Air moving faster is at a lower pressure than slower air, so the higher pressure under the wing pushes it upward. The first humans to discover how this "airfoil section" works were Australian Aborigines, when they invented the boomerang.

WHAT IS THE WORLD'S FASTEST BIRD?

People always argue about this. Most think that the peregrine falcon (right) is the fastest bird, but when its speed was accurately measured the maximum in level flight was 60 miles an hour. The world record is actually held by the Asian spine-tailed swift, which has been timed at 105 miles an hour.

❯ HOW DOES WING SHAPE AFFECT FLIGHT?

Birds' wings are shaped differently depending on how they need to fly. Fast flight demands narrow wings, such as those of swallows, while quick flight in woodland needs short, rounded wings, such as a cardinal. Falcons change the shape of their wings from long for fast flight, to swept-back for diving.

V FORMATION

A V formation, sometimes called a skein, is used by geese, ducks, and swans.

❯ WHY DO GEESE FLY IN A V?

When a bird is flying, the air just behind its wingtips swirls upward. If another bird flies in this turbulent, rising air, it can save about 15 percent of the energy it would have to use if it were flying alone. In a V formation, the leader is the only bird not saving energy: other birds take its place from time to time, to share the burden of leadership. Swans and cranes are among other birds that use this technique.

Feathers

All birds have feathers, which are essential for flight, coloration, and keeping warm and dry. Close to the bird's skin are soft down feathers to act as insulation. Stiff flight feathers on the wings and tail help birds to lift off the ground and to steer in the air.

> HOW DOES A BIRD GET WATERPROOF FEATHERS?

Birds preen, or groom themselves, mainly to keep their feathers clean, but there are other important reasons. When preening, oil from the preen gland, above the bird's tail, is spread onto the feathers to keep them waterproof. The blades of flight feathers that have become separated can be "zipped" back together by the bird's bill.

> WHAT IS MOLTING?

Growing new feathers and getting rid of old ones. As the new feathers grow, they push the old ones out of their sockets. Most birds do this once a year, but some do it twice, especially when they have different breeding and nonbreeding plumages. Many migrant birds start molting before they leave the breeding grounds, stop while they are traveling, and finish the molt when they get to the wintering area.

SWAN

The swan's stiff flight feathers were once used as quill pens. They were sharpened and dipped into ink.

HOW MANY FEATHERS DOES A BIRD HAVE?

It varies with the species and size of the bird, with its age and state of health, and with the season of the year. The smallest number was counted on a hummingbird, which had 940, and the largest on a mute swan, which had 25,216 feathers.

WHAT IS THE LINK BETWEEN FEATHERS AND DINOSAURS?

Feathers are modified scales, made from a protein called beta-keratin, which is otherwise found only in lizard skin. Birds are descended from ancient lizards related to dinosaurs. The earliest known bird, *Archaeopteryx*, had many reptilelike features.

DOWN FEATHER

Close to a bird's skin are soft down feathers to keep it warm.

FLIGHT FEATHER

A flight feather has a series of branched barbs attached to a central shaft.

DO BIRDS WEAR THERMAL UNDERWEAR?

Down feathers are the insulated underwear of birds. They are soft and fluffy, covered by a layer of windproof feathers, trapping warm air close to the bird's skin. Chicks, like those of penguins, have very thick down to keep them warm in the bitter cold of the Antarctic.

PENGUIN CHICK

This king penguin chick only has down feathers. It has not yet grown its outer, waterproof feathers.

Senses

For most birds, their sharpest sense is their eyesight. All birds use their hearing to help with communication, while birds of prey, such as owls, have supersensitive ears to home in on prey. Nearly all birds have a poor sense of smell, but some exceptions, such as kiwis, can smell food from a great distance.

OWL

Owls are nocturnal hunters. They can turn their heads 180 degrees to see behind them when they are looking for their prey.

HOMING PIGEONS

Homing pigeons are trained to find their way home over distances as long as 1,100 miles.

❯ CAN BIRDS PREDICT THE WEATHER?

Birds can sense small changes in air pressure. This may be important in predicting coming changes in the weather, which might tell them that it is time to migrate.

❯ DOES A HOMING PIGEON USE A COMPASS?

Yes! Experiments with homing pigeons, using magnets, show that they are sensitive to the earth's magnetic field, and use it to help them navigate on long journeys. Other birds probably use the same method.

➤ WHY DOES AN OWL NEED TO TURN ITS HEAD?

Owls have very large eyes to enable them to gather as much light as possible and see in the dark; but this means that they cannot move their eyes in their sockets. To compensate for this, they can turn their heads through an arc of 180 degrees.

➤ IS THE EAGLE REALLY "EAGLE-EYED"?

While it is true that birds of prey can see very well, of those that have been tested only the wedge-tailed eagle can see better than humans—two-and-a-half times better, in fact. Kestrels and falcons have about the same power of sight as we do.

WHICH BIRDS CAN SEE BEHIND THEM?

Woodcock and many ducks have their eyes placed at the sides of their heads, so that they have a 360-degree field of vision. This enables them to watch out for approaching enemies even while they are feeding.

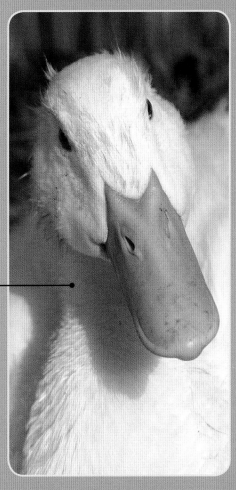

DUCK

The domestic duck is one of the few ducks that actually quacks! Most ducks make a wide range of calls, from coos to grunts.

Courtship ➤

When it comes to mating time, it is normally the female birds that take their pick among the males. To attract females, male birds may perform a courtship display. This is often a special song, but some species have developed complex displays, such as dances or fights.

➤ WHY DO BIRDS PREEN EACH OTHER?

Mutual preening helps to remove parasites, such as ticks, from places that a bird cannot reach for itself. Because the only birds that do this are members of the same family or social group, it is usually seen as part of the "bonding" process that keeps them together.

➤ WHEN DOES A FRIGATE BIRD BLOW UP?

Male frigates have a huge red throat pouch, which they inflate to attract females, making a wavering, fluting call as they do so.

➤ WHY DO BIRDS SING?

Birds do not sing because they are happy! The two main reasons are to attract a mate and to defend a territory. Birds recognize the song of their own species: females are attracted to a male with a powerful and complex song, and other males are driven away from his territory.

PEACOCK

When it wants to attract females, the male peafowl, known as a peacock, displays its gorgeous tail feathers.

> WHY DO BIRDS SHOW OFF?

For the same reasons as they sing, but with more emphasis on finding and keeping a mate. Males may display (the technical term for showing off) and even fight while the females watch. Ruffs and capercaillie perform a mass display called a lek. Afterward, the females choose the most successful males to breed with. The most elaborate displays are seen among birds-of-paradise and peacocks.

TAIL FEATHERS

When a peacock fans its tail, a pattern of fabulously colorful "eyes" can be seen.

WHICH BIRDS COLLECT RINGS FROM CANS?

To attract females, male bowerbirds in Australia and New Guinea decorate their courtship shelters (or bowers) with brightly colored flowers, seeds, and even shiny rings from discarded soft drink cans.

BRIGHT BOWER

A male bowerbird decorates its bower with objects in colors it particularly likes.

Nests and eggs

WEAVER NEST

The male African masked-weaver builds up to 25 nests each year for its series of mates.

All birds lay eggs with a hard, protective shell. Most birds keep their eggs warm by sitting on them—so that the embryo can develop—until they hatch. Eggs are usually laid in a nest, which may be a cup or dome built of twigs or leaves, a mound or burrow, or just a cleared patch of ground.

❯ WHICH BIRDS NEST IN COMMUNITIES?

Some birds, such as the sociable weavers of Africa, build huge nests occupied by as many as a hundred pairs. Other birds actually share their nests with different species. The hamerkop in East Africa builds an enormous nest, more than 3 feet across, part of which can be shared by gray kestrels and barn owls.

❯ WHICH BIRDS DIG HOLES TO NEST IN?

Many birds dig holes for their nests, including kingfishers and bank swallows in sandy banks, and woodpeckers in trees. Puffins clean out disused rabbit burrows for their nests. The quetzal in Central America scoops out a hole in a tree trunk. However they construct their nests, birds know how to do it instinctively, without being taught.

❯ WHAT IS BIRD'S NEST SOUP?

This Far Eastern delicacy is a soup made from the sticky cement that cave swiftlets use to stick twigs and feathers together to make their nests. Some species use only their saliva for this—their cement is said to be the best for making soup.

HUMMINGBIRD NEST

An Allen's hummingbird has built its nest—made of plants and feathers—on the stem of an orange.

➤ WHICH BIRDS MAKE THE BIGGEST NESTS?

Eagles. A bald eagle nest in Ohio, which was used for 35 years, was more than 8 feet across and 12 feet deep, weighing 1.8 tons. Another nest, found in Florida, was even bigger, at more than 20 feet deep.

EAGLE'S AERIE

A bald eagle's aerie, or nest, is used for many years, with more material added every year.

TOP QUESTION?

WHICH BIRD LAYS THE SMALLEST EGGS?

The smallest egg is that of the bee hummingbird, which is one-third of an inch wide and weighs less than one-fiftieth of an ounce. The egg of the emperor penguin weighs only just over 1 percent of the weight of its mother.

Raising a family >

The chicks of some species are able to fly and find some of their own food within days of being born. Other chicks remain in the nest for up to six months, being cared for by one or both parents. Even after a youngster has learned to fly, some species rely on food from their parents for a while longer.

> WHY IS IT BEST TO HATCH EARLY?

A partridge might take three weeks to lay 15 eggs, only incubating them when the last is laid, so that they all hatch together. But owls, eagles, herons, and gulls, on the other hand, incubate their eggs as soon as the first one is laid, so that the chicks hatch at different times. If food is short, the last chicks to hatch will die.

> WHAT IS AN EGG TOOTH

The hardened tip of the chick's beak is called an egg tooth. It is used to break the first hole in the eggshell just before it hatches.

BABY ROBINS

Robin chicks open their mouths wide to beg for food from their parents.

> WHEN ARE THE CHICKS BIGGER THAN THEIR PARENTS?

Shearwater chicks have to be able to survive while their parents fly far out to sea to find food, sometimes for as long as ten days. They can store fat after a meal to keep them going until the next meal. At the peak of their growth, after about 80 days, they can weigh over a pound, twice as much as their parents. They are not fed for their last ten days on the nest, so that they lose enough weight to be able to fly.

LAPWING CHICK

Lapwings are born with feathers and are able to leave the nest within a day.

> WHICH CHICKS CAN'T WAIT TO LEAVE HOME?

Lapwings are a good example of "nest-leaving" chicks: they leave the nest as soon as they can walk, within hours of hatching—but still in the company of a parent. "Nest-living" chicks stay much longer in the case of macaws, for as long as three months.

TOP QUESTION ?

WHICH PARENT INCUBATES THE EGGS?

In most species, incubation—or sitting on the eggs (right)—is shared between both parents. But in polygamous species, where males have several mates, incubation is the female's job.

Getting food

Different species of birds have a wide range of diets, from nectar, fruit, plants, or seeds to other animals, including birds. A bird's beak, feet, and wings are well suited to finding its food. For example, penguins chase their fish prey underwater, using their wings and webbed feet to power along.

WHAT IS A BIRD PELLET?

The indigestible remains of a bird's food, such as bones and shells, wrapped in softer leftovers, such as fur or wool. The bird throws up these neat packages, instead of trying to pass them through its gut.

DO BIRDS USE TOOLS?

Yes. Woodpecker finches use cactus spines to pry out larvae from their burrows in dead wood. Egyptian vultures pick up stones and drop them on ostrich eggs to break them. Green-backed herons have been seen using bread as bait to catch fish.

TOP QUESTION

HOW DO BIRDS CATCH FISH?

With their beaks—which often have a hooked tip or jagged edges to help them grip their prey—or with their feet, such as fish eagles or ospreys. As well as long, curved talons, the feet often have roughened soles to improve the grip. The African fish eagle strikes its prey with its long hind talon and then clenches the others around it.

OSPREY WITH FISH

When it sights a fish, the osprey plunges feet first into the water, diving up to 3 feet down.

➤ WHY DON'T WOODPECKERS GET HEADACHES?

Woodpeckers (right) drill the bark of trees looking for insects. They use their head as a hammer and their beak as a chisel, but the soft, spongy bone between the beak and the skull absorbs the impact.

➤ HOW DO JAYS AND OAK TREES HELP EACH OTHER?

As well as preying on the chicks of other birds, jays feed on acorns. In fall, when acorns are plentiful, jays bury some of them to dig up later. Those that they don't find will grow into new oak trees.

BLUE JAY

The blue jay has a strong beak for cracking nuts and eating insects, grain, and seeds.

Migration >

Some bird species make a yearly migration to find different weather conditions in another part of the world. Many birds spend their spring and summer in temperate or polar regions, where they breed. In the winter, they may move to tropical regions to find warmer weather.

> HOW DO BIRDS KNOW WHEN TO LEAVE?

Some ducks migrate only when the weather really turns cold, but most birds leave long before winter comes: Marsh warblers migrate in July. Their bodies tell them when to go, as changes in hormones cause them to put on fat ready for the journey. The final trigger to move is when the days start to get shorter in fall.

GEESE

The white-fronted goose breeds in Arctic Canada or Siberia. It spends the winter much farther south, in the United States or Japan.

> HOW FAST DO BIRDS FLY?

Studies using radar show that small birds, such as warblers, move at around 20 miles an hour when they are migrating, and ducks at around 40 miles an hour. They usually fly for only 6 or 8 hours a day, but one small bird (see p. 214) in England was found in Liberia, Africa, 3,500 miles away, only eight days later. It had covered around 430 miles a day, traveling for ten hours every day.

> WHY DO SOME BIRDS MIGRATE SO FAR?

To move out of areas which are suitable for breeding back to places where they can survive the winter. The reason for moving back to the breeding area is usually because it contains plenty of food in the summer to feed the chicks.

➤ WHY DO SOME BIRDS STAY BEHIND?

In Sweden, female and young chaffinches migrate south in winter, but some males stay behind in their breeding territories. European blackbirds (left) do the same. It seems that the males stay behind throughout the winter to hold onto the best breeding territories.

TOP QUESTION ?

WHAT BIRD LIVES IN CONSTANT SUMMER?

The Arctic tern (below) breeds in the Arctic during the northern hemisphere's summer, then migrates every year to spend the southern hemisphere's summer in the Antarctic, a total distance of 23,800 miles between breeding seasons.

Flightless birds >

About 60 species of bird are flightless. Instead, they rely on their ability to run or swim. The ostrich family contains the biggest flightless birds, including emus, rheas, and cassowaries. Penguins, which live in the southern hemisphere, are the most numerous flightless birds.

> WHY ARE SOME BIRDS PART-TIME FLIERS?

Because they give up flying when they molt. Geese that breed in the high Arctic can escape from the few predators that live there by swimming, so they can change all their wing feathers at once while their goslings are growing theirs. When the time comes to fly south for the winter, the whole family has new flight feathers.

TOP QUESTION

?

WHICH BIRD IS LIKE A BANDICOOT?

A bandicoot is a small insect-eating mammal living in the forests of Australia and New Guinea. But New Zealand has no native mammals, and the job of forest-floor insect eater has been taken over by the flightless kiwi (left).

➤ WHICH BIRD FLIES UNDERWATER?

Penguins are wonderful fliers. Their narrow, sharp-edge wings are like those of a swift, and their streamlined bodies allow them to move very fast and maneuver with great precision. The only reason we call them "flightless" is that they do it underwater.

➤ WHY DOES A CASSOWARY WEAR A HELMET?

It needs one to protect its head from thorns and branches as it dashes through the forest. All that remains of its flight feathers are bare black spines, curving around its body. They also protect it by brushing aside vines and bushes.

➤ HOW FAST CAN AN OSTRICH RUN?

A biologist once drove alongside a running ostrich on the Mara Plains in Kenya with his speedometer reading 40 miles an hour.

OSTRICH

The ostrich, which lives in Africa, has the fastest land speed of any bird. It eats seeds, plants, and insects.

Birds and other animals

Some birds have learned to live closely with other animals and to benefit from a relationship with them. This is called a symbiotic relationship. The relationship between birds and humans is ancient. Ducks and chickens may be kept by humans for their meat and eggs. Parrots and canaries may be kept as pets. But, sometimes, birds are just seen as pests.

HOW CAN A BIRD BRING DOWN A JET PLANE?

The greatest danger is that a large bird, or a flock of small ones, such as starlings, might be sucked into the air intake of the engine, causing it to stop. But sometimes a bird crashes through the cockpit windshield and injures the pilot.

WHAT IS A HONEYGUIDE?

A small African bird that feeds on bee larvae, honey, and beeswax from wild bees' nests. It has learned to show humans as well as ratels (or honeybadgers) where bees' nests are by fluttering around them and calling until they follow it. When the ratel or the human breaks open the nest to get the honey, the honeyguide has a free feed.

BLUETIT

Scientists think that bluetits taught each other how to break through foil milk bottle-tops by watching repeated attempts.

➤ WHICH BIRDS ENJOY A DAILY PINT?

This habit of bluetits was first noticed in 1929, in England, when milk began to be delivered in bottles with foil tops. No one knows how the first bluetit discovered how to get at the creamy milk, but before long they were doing it all over the country.

WHY DO BIRDS PERCH ON RHINOS?

Oxpeckers, or tickbirds, are members of the starling family that feed only on the skin parasites of large mammals. They have very sharp beaks and claws. All large mammals put up with their scratchy feet—and their habit of pulling out hair to line their nests—because they remove troublesome parasites.

CROWS

Crows follow behind a plow to catch worms and other insects in the churned-up soil.

➤ WHY DO CROWS FOLLOW THE PLOW?

Crows do this because they have learned that, as the plow turns over the soil, it exposes lots of good things to eat.

Studying birds >

Someone who studies birds is called an ornithologist. Ornithology tells us about the behavior and evolution of birds, as well as their importance to the environment. Many people also bird-watch just for the pleasure.

> HOW DO YOU COUNT BIRDS?

There are many ways. One method is to attach a small numbered metal or plastic ring to a bird's leg (right) or wing so that it can be recognized when it is later recaptured. Other methods just involve close watching. The most reliable way to study bird populations is during the breeding season, when the adults are busy at their nests.

> WHAT IS A SONOGRAM?

This is a means of printing out the sounds birds make so that they can be studied. A sonogram shows the frequency of the sound and the time it lasts. This allows scientists to identify different courtship and territorial calls and songs.

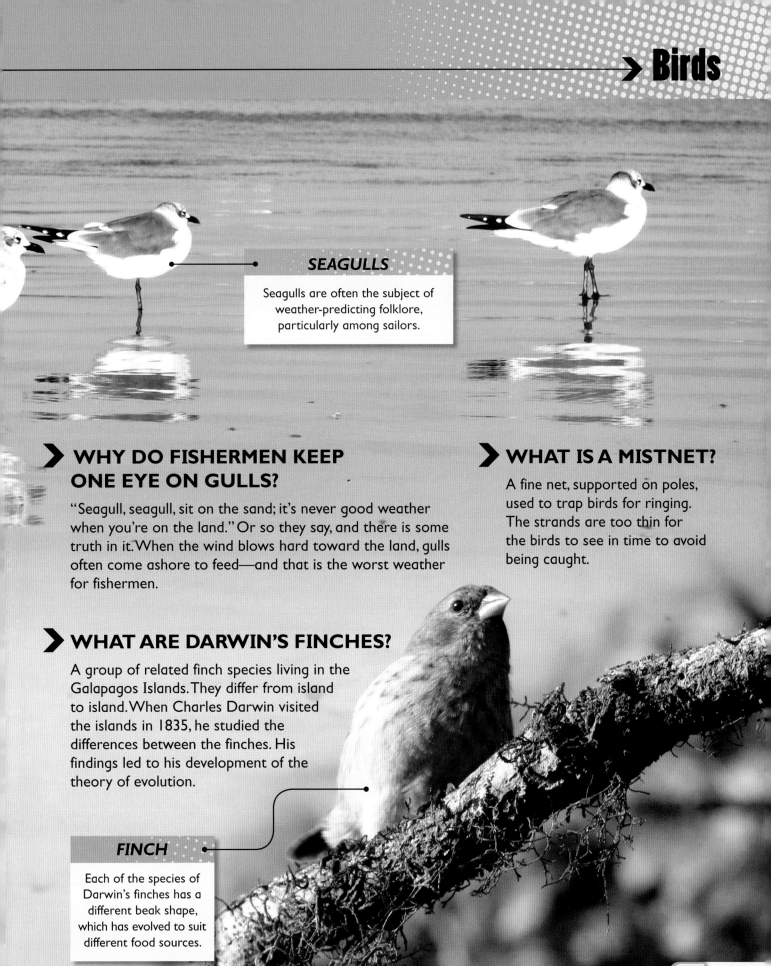

SEAGULLS

Seagulls are often the subject of weather-predicting folklore, particularly among sailors.

> WHY DO FISHERMEN KEEP ONE EYE ON GULLS?

"Seagull, seagull, sit on the sand; it's never good weather when you're on the land." Or so they say, and there is some truth in it. When the wind blows hard toward the land, gulls often come ashore to feed—and that is the worst weather for fishermen.

> WHAT IS A MISTNET?

A fine net, supported on poles, used to trap birds for ringing. The strands are too thin for the birds to see in time to avoid being caught.

> WHAT ARE DARWIN'S FINCHES?

A group of related finch species living in the Galapagos Islands. They differ from island to island. When Charles Darwin visited the islands in 1835, he studied the differences between the finches. His findings led to his development of the theory of evolution.

FINCH

Each of the species of Darwin's finches has a different beak shape, which has evolved to suit different food sources.

Glossary

Aquatic
Something that lives in water.

Artery
Blood vessel that carries blood away from the heart.

Asteroid
A piece of rock in the solar system, varying in size from a grain of dust to hundreds of miles across.

Atmosphere
A layer of gas held around a planet by gravity. The Earth's atmosphere is over 500 miles thick.

Atom
Once thought to be the smallest part of a substance. We now know that atoms are made up of smaller parts known as subatomic particles.

Beak

The jaws of a bird, made of bone, which it uses for feeding.

Camouflage
Coloring that allows an animal to blend in with its background.

Cell
The tiny unit from which all bodies are made. The smallest animals have just one cell, and the largest have many millions.

Climate
The pattern of weather in an area. Plants and animals are suited to their native climate.

Colony
A group of animals living together in a shared home.

Conifer
A tree that has needle-shape leaves.

Crustacean
An animal without a backbone that has a body covered by an outer skeleton. Crustaceans include crabs, lobsters, crayfish, shrimp, krill, and barnacles.

Desert
An area of land that receives little rain. As life needs water to survive, fewer plants and animals live in deserts.

Diaphragm
The dome-shape sheet of muscle that lies beneath the lungs. During breathing, the diaphragm flattens to increase the volume of the lungs and to pull air into them.

Digestion
The process of breaking down food into very small particles in the body. They can then pass into the blood to provide the body with all the substances it needs to stay healthy.

DNA
Short for deoxyribonucleic acid. DNA is arranged in a twin spiral shape, called a double helix, and contains the genetic instructions for every cell.

Electricity
The movement of tiny particles called electrons through a substance, such as metal. This causes an electrical current that can be used as a source of power.

Electron
A subatomic particle. Along with protons and neutrons, electrons make up atoms. Electrons have a negative electrical charge and play a vital role in electricity and magnetism.

Endangered
A species, or kind, of animal that is so few in number that it is in danger of disappearing.

Equator
An imaginary line that runs around the middle of the earth.

Evaporate
To change from a liquid into a gas, for instance when water turns into steam in a boiling saucepan.

Evolution
The process by which animals and plants adapt and change over many generations. Those that are best suited to their

surroundings survive and produce young, while others die out.

Extinction

When a species can no longer survive due to overhunting or when there is a change in its habitat, such as deforestation or climate change.

Feces

Waste products left over from the digestive system.

Fin

A part of the body of a fish that is used for swimming.

Force

A push or a pull that makes an object speed up or slow down.

Galaxy

A group of millions of stars held together by gravity.

Gravity

The force of attraction between any two objects, such as the pull between the earth and the moon.

Greenhouse effect

The warming of the Earth, also known as "global warming," due to the presence of the gas carbon dioxide in the air, which stops heat escaping from the atmosphere. Pollution from burning oil and coal is causing an increase in the greenhouse effect.

Habitat

The place where an animal or plant lives.

Herbivore

An animal that eats only plants.

Herd

A large group of hoofed mammals that live together.

Hibernation

A sleep that some animals go into to survive the winter. The animal's heart rate slows down.

Ice caps

The layers of ice and snow that cover the North and South poles.

Mammal

An animal with a backbone that usually has hair on its skin. Female mammals make milk to feed their young.

Migration

A regular journey made by an animal.

Molecule

Tiny particle that makes up a substance. A molecule can be as small as just two atoms held together by a chemical bond.

Moon

A planet's natural satellite.

Muscle

A part of the body that is able to contract (shorten) and relax (lengthen) to produce movement.

Nerve
A bundle of fibers in the body that carries electrical signals to and from the brain.

Neutron
A subatomic particle found in the nucleus of an atom. Neutrons carry no electrical charge.

Organ
A part of an animal or plant that performs a particular task. The heart, for example, pumps blood around the body.

Plankton
The tiny plants and animals that are found floating close to the surface of ponds, lakes, and seas.

Polar
Related to the cold areas around the North and South poles.

Predator
An animal that hunts and eats other animals.

Prey
An animal that is hunted by another animal for food.

Proton
A subatomic particle found in the nucleus of an atom. Protons carry a positive electrical charge.

Rain forest
Dense forest found in areas with high rainfall around the equator.

Satellite
Any object that orbits a planet, held by the planet's gravity.

Senses
The ways humans and animals are able to experience the world around them. Humans have five senses: sight, hearing, touch, smell, and taste.

Skeleton
The framework of a body that holds it together. Some skeletons are inside the body, while others are outside.

Solar System
The part of space that includes the Sun, the planets that circle the Sun, and all the moons and asteroids in between.

Temperate
Areas of the world that have a mild climate and four seasons.

Tropical
Areas of the world that lie around the middle of the Earth, near the equator, and are hot all year round.

Vein
Blood vessel that carries blood back to the heart. The larger veins have valves inside them to stop blood flowing the wrong way.

Venom
A harmful liquid that some animals make to kill prey or to defend themselves.

Vertebrate
Any animal that has a bony skeleton and a backbone. Animals without a backbone are called invertebrate.

Index ➤

Acknowledgments

t = top, b = bottom, l = left, r = right, m = middle

1 Wei Send Chen/Dreamstime.com, 2 Richard Griffin/Dreamstime.com, 3 Sebastian Kaulitzki/Dreamstime.com, 4–5 Mark Karasek/Dreamstime.com, 6–7 Luke Pederson/Dreamstime.com, 8–9 ESA/NASA/SOHO/JPL, 10 NASA/JPL/Caltech, 11t Eraxion/Dreamstime.com, 11b NASA, 12 ESA/NASA/SOHO, 12–13 Girts Pavlins/Dreamstime.com, 13 Laurent Dambies/Dreamstime.com, 14 NASA, 15l NASA/JPL/USGS, 16l NASA, 16r Liaj/Dreamstime.com, 17 Johnny Lye/Dreamstime.com, 18 NASA, 19l and b Steve Albers/NASA, 19r Hinode JAXA/NASA/PPARC, 20–21 Luke Pederson/Dreamstime.com, 21t Marbo/Dreamstime.com, 21m Hinode JAXA/NASA, 21b NASA/SOHO, 22–23 NASA/JPL, 22 Beriliu/Dreamstime.com, 23 NASA/JPL/Caltech, 24–25t NASA/JPL/USGS, 24–25b NASA/JPL/Arizona State University, 25 and 26 NASA/JPL, 27t NASA/JPL/University of Arizona, 27b NASA/JPL, 28–29 NASA, 29t NASA/JPL, 29b NASA/JPL/University of Colorado, 30 and 31l NASA, 31t NASA/JPL/Caltech, 31r ESO/Getty Images, 32–33 David Gilder/Dreamstime.com, 32 NASA, 33l T. Rector (University of Alaska Anchorage), Z. Levay and L. Frattare (Space Telescope Science Institute) and National Optical Astronomy Observatory/Association of Universities for Research in Astronomy/National Science Foundation, 33r NASA Johnson Space Center, 34–35 NASA/ESA, 36 COBE Project/DMR/NASA, 37l and r NASA/Adolf Schaller for STScI, 38 and 39t NASA/ESA, 39b NASA/JPL/Caltech/SSC, 40–41 Andreus/Dreamstime.com, 41t Fermi National Accelerator Laboratory, 41b United States Federal Government, 42 NASA/Jeff Hester and Paul Scowen Arizona State University, 43t NASA/JPL/Hubble, 43bl NICMOS Group (STScI, ESA)/NICMOS Science Team (University of Arizona)/NASA, 43bm JPL/NASA/NOAO/ESA and The Hubble Heritage Team (STScI/AURA), 43br NASA/C.R. O'Dell and S.K. Wong (Rice University), 44l Serge Brunier/NASA, 44r Thomas Tuchan/iStockphoto, 45 NASA/ESA/Hubble Heritage (STScI/AURA)-ESA/Hubble Collaboration, 46–47 Manfred Konrad/iStockphoto, 46 URA/STScI/NASA/JPL, 47 NASA/ESA/A. Field (STScI), 48 NASA/J. P. Harrington and K. J. Borkowski University of Maryland, 49t NASA/JPL/Caltech, 49b NASA/ESA, 50t NASA, 50b NASA/ESA/AURA/Caltech, 51 Shaun Lowe/iStockphoto, 52t NASA, 52b and 53 NASA/ESA/The Hubble Heritage Team (STScI/AURA), 54–55 HST/NASA/ESA, 55l NASA/JPL/Caltech, 55r Dave Long/iStockphoto, 56t NASA/CXC/SAO, 56b J. Bahcall (IAS, Princeton)/M. Disney (Univ. Wales)/NASA, 57 Manfred Konrad/iStockphoto, 58–59 Endi Dewata/iStockphoto, 59l NASA/JPL, 59r NASA, 60–61 SMC Images/Getty Images, 62–63 Fabrizio Zanier/iStockphoto, 63t Dorling Kindersley/Getty Images, 63b Getty Images, 64–65 Tatiana Nikolaevna Kalashnikova/Dreamstime.com, 65t Photowitch/Dreamstime.com, 65b Topical Press Agency/Getty Images, 66 Mark Schneider/Getty Images, 66–67 Ian Wilson/Dreamstime.com, 67 Hulton Archive/Getty Images, 68–69 Panoramic Images/Getty Images, 69l Sergey Rogovets/Dreamstime.com, 69r Johnny Lye/Dreamstime.com, 70 NASA/MSFC, 71l Kelpfi sh/Dreamstime.com, 71r Mat Monteith/Dreamstime.com, 72–73 Yory Frenklakh/Dreamstime.com, 72 Ivan Mateev/iStockphoto, 73 Vladimir Lukovic/Dreamstime.com, 74 Zoom-zoom/Dreamstime.com, 75l iStockphoto, 76l Rade Lukovic/iStockphoto, 76r Ilya Rabkin/Dreamstime.com, 77t Ken Lucas/Getty Images, 77b Victor Boswell/National Geographic/Getty Images, 78 Andrea Danti/Dreamstime.com, 79t Dobresum/iStockphoto, 79b AFP/Getty Images, 80–81 Andrew Edelstein/iStockphoto, 81t Darren Baker/Dreamstime.com, 81b Trevor Fisher/iStockphoto, 82–83 Sebastian Kaulitzki/Dreamstime.com, 83t Martin McCarthy/iStockphoto, 83b Dan McCoy/Rainbow/Getty Images, 84–85 Lance Michaels/Dreamstime.com, 84 David Hancock/Dreamstime.com, 85 Oliver Sun Kim/iStockphoto, 86–87 Oli Tennent/Getty Images, 88 NASA, 89t David Coleman/Dreamstime.com, 89b Jeff Hower/iStockphoto, 90–91t Brandon Laufenberg/iStockphoto, 90–91b Rafa Irusta/iStockphoto, 91 Marcin Kempski/iStockphoto, 92l Steven Wynn/iStockphoto, 92r Anders Aagesen/iStockphoto, 93t Romilly Lockyer/Getty Images, 93b Gabigarcia/Dreamstime.com, 94 and 95b NASA, 95t Drazen Vukelic/Dreamstime.com, 96t Andrey Pali/Dreamstime.com, 96b Andra Cerar/Dreamstime.com, 96–97 Jinyoung Lee/Dreamstime.com, 97 Chiya Li/Dreamstime.com, 98 Richard Griffin/Dreamstime.com, 98–99 Gary Vestal/Getty Images, 99 Norman Pogson/Dreamstime.com, 100l Paul Phillips/Dreamstime.com, 100r Adam Gryko/Dreamstime.com, 101l Katharina Wittfeld/Dreamstime.com, 101r Lukasz Tymszan/Dreamstime.com, 102 Cammeraydave/Dreamstime.com, 103 Gofer/Dreamstime.com, 104 Feng Yu/Dreamstime.com, 104–105 Martin Eaves/Dreamstime.com, 105 Shannon Neal/Dreamstime.com, 106 Josef Bosak/Dreamstime.com, 107t Francis Black/Dreamstime.com, 107b Hong Siew Mee/Dreamstime.com, 108 iStockphoto, 109t Irochka/Dreamstime.com, 109b Dreamstime.com, 110 Pixhook/iStockphoto, 111 Javarman/Dreamstime.com, 112–113 Peter Dazeley/Getty Images, 114 Dr. Don Fawcett/Getty Images, 115t Clouds Hill Imaging Ltd/Corbis, 115b Anette Linnea Rasmussen/Dreamstime.com, 116 3D4Medical.com/Getty Images, 117l Carolina K. Smith M.D./Dreamstime.com, 117r Peterfactors/Dreamstime.com, 118 3D4Medical.com/Getty Images, 119t Bobby Deal/Dreamstime.com, 119b Emir Memedovski/Dreamstime.com, 120 Dannyphoto80/Dreamstime.com, 121l Andres Balcazar/iStockphoto, 121r Sebastian Kaulitzki/Dreamstime.com, 122 Tihis/Dreamstime.com, 122–123 Dan McCoy/Rainbow/Getty Images, 123 Ryszard Bednarek/Dreamstime.com, 124 Kutay Tanir/iStockphoto, 125t Dannyphoto80/Dreamstime.com, 125b Rosemarie Gearhart/iStockphoto, 126l David Davis/Dreamstime.com, 126r Gordana Sermek/Dreamstime.com, 127 3D4Medical.com/Getty Images, 128 Visuals Unlimited/Corbis, 129l Tracy Hebden/iStockphoto, 129r Oguzaral/Dreamstime.com, 130–131 Kennan Harvey/Getty Images, 131t Vlad Turchenko/Dreamstime.com, 131b 3D4Medical.com/Getty Images, 132–133 Sebastian Kaulitzki/Dreamstime.com, 133l Sgame/Dreamstime.com, 133r Dannyphoto80/Dreamstime.com, 134 Sebastian Kaulitzki/Dreamstime.com, 134–135 Pete Saloutos/Corbis, 135 Stephen Coburn/Dreamstime.com, 136–137 Devan Muir/iStockphoto, 137l Jenna Duetsch/iStockphoto, 137r Koi88/Dreamstime.com, 138–139 J.A. Kraulis/All Canada Photos/Getty Images, 140–141 Henk Van Mierlo/Dreamstime.com, 141t Dmitry Pichugin/Dreamstime.com, 141b iStockphoto, 142–143 Eric Isselée/Dreamstime.com, 143l Pixelite/Dreamstime.com, 143r Jim Parkin/Dreamstime.com, 144t Sburel/Dreamstime.com, 144b Robert F. Sisson/National Geographic/Getty Images, 144–145 Dmitry Pichugin/Dreamstime.com, 146–147 Uwe Halstenbach/iStockphoto, 146 Diane Diederich/iStockphoto, 147 Mark Atkins/Dreamstime.com, 148–149 David Ciemny/iStockphoto, 148 Vincent Vanweddingen/iStockphoto, 149 Eric Boucher/Dreamstime.com, 150 Julia Britvich/Dreamstime.com, 151t Avner Richard/Dreamstime.com, 151b Carmentianya/Dreamstime.com, 152–153 Sergey Anatolievich/Dreamstime.com, 152 Gail Johnson/Dreamstime.com, 153 Lauren Jones/Dreamstime.com, 154–155 Andrei Calangiu/Dreamstime.com, 155t Simone van den Berg/Dreamstime.com, 155b Christophe D./Dreamstime.com, 156t Geopappas/Dreamstime.com, 156b Tom Davison/Dreamstime.com, 157 Bronwyn8/Dreamstime.com, 158 Kenneth McIntosh/iStockphoto, 159t Vinicius Tupinamba/Dreamstime.com, 159b Tradkelly/Dreamstime.com, 160 Joseph C. Justice Jr./iStockphoto, 161l Co Rentmeester/Time & Life Pictures/Getty Images, 161r iStockphoto, 162–163t Kai Zhang/Dreamstime.com, 162–163b Deborah Benbrook/Dreamstime.com, 163 Kwest19/Dreamstime.com, 164–165 Stephen Frink/Getty Images, 166–167 iStockphoto, 167t 2005 Richard Ling, 167b Dennis Sabo/Dreamstime.com, 168–169 Harald Bolten/Dreamstime.com, 169t Stephen Frink/Getty Images, 169b Anthony Hall/Dreamstime.com, 170 Peter Pinnock/Getty Images, 171t Peter David/Getty Images, 171b Reinhard Dirscherl/Getty Images, 172t Tom_robbrecht/Dreamstime.com, 172b Asther Lau Choon Siew/Dreamstime.com, 173 Stacy Barnett/Dreamstime.com, 174 Gary Bell/zefa/Corbis, 175t Ligio/Dreamstime.com, 175b Asther Lau Choon Siew/Dreamstime.com, 176t Gert Very/Dreamstime.com, 176b Steffen Foerster/Dreamstime.com, 177 Zepherwind/Dreamstime.com, 178–179 Andreas Tille/GNU, 178 Arthur Morris/Corbis, 179 Bill Curtsinger/National Geographic/Getty Images, 180–181 Matthias Weinrich/Dreamstime.com, 180 Regien Paassen/Dreamstime.com, 181 Asther Lau Choon Siew/Dreamstime.com, 182 Albert Cheng/iStockphoto, 183t Dejan Sarman/iStockphoto, 183b Wei Send Chen/Dreamstime.com, 184t Susan McManus/iStockphoto, 184b NOAA, 185 Yulia Birzhanova/Dreamstime.com, 186 Carol Buchanan/Dreamstime.com, 186–187 Denis Scott/Corbis, 187 Ian Scott/Dreamstime.com, 188–189 Brett Atkins/Dreamstime.com, 189t David Schrader/Dreamstime.com, 189b Blphotocorp/Dreamstime.com, 190–191 Grant Faint/Image Bank/Getty Images, 192 MDF/GNU, 192–193 Armin Rose/Dreamstime.com, 193 Andreas Resch/Dreamstime.com, 194 KTS/Dreamstime.com, 195t John Pitcher/iStockphoto, 195b Gino Santa Maria/Dreamstime.com, 196 Jaroslaw Brzychcy/Dreamstime.com, 197l Feng Yu/Dreamstime.com, 197m Pixhook/iStockphoto, 197r Jeremy Wee/Dreamstime.com, 198 Dariusz Miszkiel/Dreamstime.com, 198–199 Chris Zwaenepoel/Dreamstime.com, 199 Olga Prokopova/Dreamstime.com, 200 John Loader/Dreamstime.com, 200–201 Mark Karasek/Dreamstime.com, 201 Martin Harvey/Corbis, 202 Johannes Gerhardus Swanepoel/Dreamstime.com, 203t Brian Grant/Dreamstime.com, 203b George D. Lepp/Corbis, 204 Maunger/Dreamstime.com, 205t Vchphoto/Dreamstime.com, 205b Steve Brace, 206 Steve Byland/Dreamstime.com, 207t Npage/Dreamstime.com, 207b Frank Cezus/Getty Images, 208–209 Eric Gevaert/Dreamstime.com, 209t Brian Lambert/Dreamstime.com, 209b Roy Longmuir/Dreamstime.com, 210 Maungatautari Ecological Island Trust, 210–211 Olga Solovei/Dreamstime.com, 211 Lu Zhang/Dreamstime.com, 212–213 Constantin Opris/Dreamstime.com, 213l Kim Taylor/Dorling Kindersley/Getty Images, 213r Chris Fourie/Dreamstime.com, 214–215 Norbert Rehm/Dreamstime.com, 214 Svetlana Kashkina/Dreamstime.com, 215 Morten Elm/Dreamstime.com, 216t NASA Johnson Space Center, 216b Armin Rose/Dreamstime.com, 217 Gabigarcia/Dreamstime.com, 218 Kenneth McIntosh/iStockphoto.